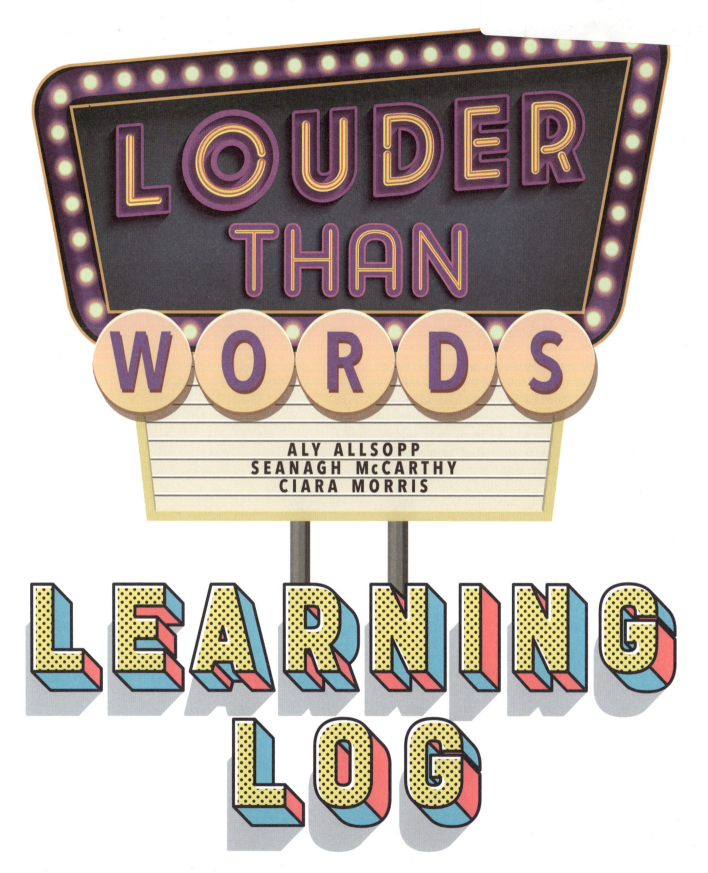

PUBLISHED BY:
Educate.ie

Walsh Educational Books Ltd
Castleisland, Co. Kerry, Ireland

www.educate.ie

DESIGN:
Liz White Designs

LAYOUT:
Jen Patton

PRINTED AND BOUND BY:
Walsh Colour Print, Castleisland

© Aly Allsopp, Seanagh McCarthy, Ciara Morris, 2022

Without limiting the rights under copyright, this book is sold subject to the condition that it shall not, by way of trade or otherwise, be reproduced, stored in or introduced into a retrieval system, or transmitted, in any form or by any means (electronic, mechanical, photocopying, recording or otherwise), or otherwise circulated, without the publisher's prior consent, in any form other than that in which it is published and without a similar condition, including this condition, being imposed on the subsequent publisher. The author and publisher have made every effort to trace all copyright holders, but if some have been inadvertently overlooked, we would be happy to make the necessary arrangements at the first opportunity.

ISBN: 978-1-913698-84-3

COPYRIGHT PERMISSIONS:
Excerpts from AMERICAN BORN CHINESE by Gene Luen Yang. Copyright © 2006 by Gene Yang. Reprinted by permission of First Second, an imprint of Roaring Brook Press, a division of Holtzbrinck Publishing Holdings Limited Partnership. All Rights Reserved; Special Olympics Ireland; Shutterstock

Contents

1 Get to Grips with ... Features and Terms 1
- Features 1
- Literary Terms 4
  - Poetic Devices 4
  - Fiction 5
  - Drama 5
  - Shakespearean Drama 6
  - Film 6

2 Collect and Reflect 7
- **UNIT 1** Safe Spaces 7
- **UNIT 2** Consideration and Compassion 16
- **UNIT 3** Sense and Sustainability 21
- **UNIT 4** Empower and Engage 29
- **UNIT 5** Fast Forward 40
- **UNIT 6** Courageous Creativity 48
- **UNIT 7** Influence and Inform 58
- **UNIT 8** Truth and Trust 66
- **UNIT 9** Animated Adventures 73
- **UNIT 10** Individuals and Identities 79
- **UNIT 11** Power and Powerlessness 85
- **UNIT 12** Stand Up, Speak Out! 93

3 Fire Ahead with Assessment 101

Introduction

Welcome to your *Louder than Words* Learning Log, where you will:

- revise and record the features and terms related to the different genres of literature you study during Junior Cycle English
- complete Get Creative tasks
- reflect on texts you have read and on tasks and units you have completed
- find advice and ideas for Classroom-Based and Final Assessment
- answer past paper and exam-style questions

1 Get to grips with ... FEATURES AND TERMS

Features

Genre	Features/Format/Layout	Language style
Diary entry	<ul><li>Detailed account of events</li><li>'Dear Diary' format</li><li>Date and references to place/time</li><li>Description of feelings</li></ul>	<ul><li>Informal register</li><li>First person (personal pronoun 'I')</li><li>Conversational tone</li><li>Private/intimate tone</li></ul>
Review	<ul><li>Information, overview and recommendation</li><li>Details, information and facts</li><li>Honest opinions</li></ul>	<ul><li>Persuasive language</li><li>First person ('I')</li><li>Balanced</li></ul>
Open letter	<ul><li>Date</li><li>Greeting</li><li>Sign-off</li><li>Addresses not required</li></ul>	<ul><li>Informative</li><li>Persuasive (raising awareness or gaining support)</li></ul>
Personal essay	<ul><li>Clear purpose</li><li>Introduction, main content and conclusion</li><li>Thoughts, feelings, reflections and insights</li><li>Information and facts (if applicable)</li></ul>	<ul><li>First person (personal pronoun 'I')</li><li>Personal experiences and anecdotes</li><li>Thoughts, feelings, reactions and comments</li><li>Reflective tone</li></ul>
Online article	<ul><li>Headline</li><li>By-line</li><li>Date</li><li>Information – facts, figures and statistics</li><li>Quotations</li><li>Time stamp</li><li>Interactive features – comments and feedback</li><li>Links to social media</li></ul>	<ul><li>Objective (news)</li><li>Subjective (feature)</li><li>Informative style</li><li>Interactive</li><li>Entertaining</li></ul>
Email	<ul><li>Sender's email</li><li>Recipient's email</li><li>Subject</li><li>Date</li><li>Greeting</li><li>Sign-off</li></ul>	<ul><li>Paragraphs</li><li>Clear purpose</li><li>Appropriate tone and register (formal or informal)</li></ul>

Louder than Words >> Learning Log

Genre	Features/Format/Layout	Language style
Visual text	- Background, foreground and centre - Colour - Images - Focus	- Analysis of subject and theme - Perspective of reader - Tone
Speech	- Address to audience - Clear introduction/outline of main argument - Statistics - Cultural references - Personal experiences and anecdotes	- Inclusive (personal pronouns 'you', 'we', 'our') - Rhetorical questions - Informative style - Objective tone - Emphatic language
Blog	- Name of blog - Name of blogger - Post heading - Opinions - Details of events - Date and time stamps - Interactive features	- Informal register - First person (personal pronoun 'I') - Language appropriate to the topic and audience
Short story	- Setting: where and when - Plot: situation, conflict, rising action, climax, falling action, ending - Characterisation: development of characters	- Use of the senses (sights, sounds, smells, touch, feelings) - Descriptive (use of adjectives, adverbs, metaphors, colours) - Show, don't tell!
Formal letter	- Address (recipient) Address (sender) - Greeting - Date - Paragraphs - Sign-off	- Formal tone - Focus on purpose of the letter - Polite and direct
Advertising	- Imagery - Slogan - Caption - Copy - Logo - Endorsement - Hashtags and links	- Informative - Persuasive - Eye-catching and attention grabbing - Clearly directed at target audience
Podcast	- Introduction - Script format (not dialogue) - Conclusion - Interviews - Advertising	- Addresses listeners - Clear purpose - Personal experience and anecdotes - Informative and educational - Entertaining

1 » Get to grips with ... Features and Terms

Genre	Features/Format/Layout	Language style
Informal letter	- Address (recipient) - Greeting - Date - Paragraphs - Sign-off	- Informal, conversational register - Focus on the purpose of the letter
Biography	- Detailed description of the person - Insight - Quotes - Facts and achievements	- Third-person (personal pronouns 'he', 'she', 'they') - Informative - Accurate - Descriptive - Personal
Debate	- Introduction - Greeting - Motion - Rebuttal - Conclusion	- Inclusive (personal pronouns 'you', 'we', 'our') - Rhetorical questions - Informative - Persuasive - Emphatic
Interview	- Transcript or feature - Questions and answers - Direct quotes and/or summarised answers - Pull quotes	- Clear purpose - Open-ended questions - Reported speech - Probing - Observational
Autobiography	- Personal details and experiences - Facts and information - Chronological narrative	- First person (personal pronoun 'I') - Honest and open tone - Descriptive
Guidelines	- List of materials or equipment - Step-by-step instructions - Supporting images - Practical advice and support	- Informative - Easy to follow - Imperative verbs - Clear and direct

Literary Terms

Poetic devices

Term	Definition	Example
Alliteration		
Imagery		
Onomatopoeia		
Rhyme		
Theme		
Metaphor		
Repetition		
Simile		
Tone		
Mood		
Voice		
Enjambment		
Satire		
Hyperbole		
Parody		
Irony		
Sibilance		
Personification		
Allusion		
Assonance		

1 » Get to grips with ... Features and Terms

Fiction

Term	Definition	Example
Opening line		
Narrative voice		
Setting		
Plot structure		
Characterisation		
Flashback		
Foreshadowing		
Blurb		
Prologue		
Key moment		

Drama

Term	Definition	Example
Props		
Stage directions		
Sound effects		
Register		
Stagecraft		
Dialogue		
Monologue		

Louder than Words >> Learning Log

Shakespearean Drama

Term	Definition	Example
Aside		
Comic relief		
Dramatic irony		
Exit		
Exeunt		
Monologue		
Soliloquy		

Film

Term	Definition	Term	Definition
Trailer		Zooming	
Establishing shot		Fade	
High-angle shot		Jump cut	
Low-angle shot		Lighting	
Point-of-view shot		Score	
Close-up shot		Diegetic sound	
Tracking		Non-diegetic sound	
Panning		Screenplay	

2 Collect and Reflect
UNIT 1 Safe Spaces

GET CREATIVE

Read the diary entry on page 4 of your textbook. Imagine what might happen next in the fish scandal and write the subsequent diary entry from Hendrik's perspective.

Louder than Words >> Learning Log

REFLECT ON IT

Read the three student reflections on the extract from *Word Nerd* by Susin Nielsen on page 7 of your textbook.

Tick the reflection that you feel best captures your response to the following question: **Did you enjoy reading the piece?**

Megan: I felt so sorry for Ambrose! Those bullies are so cruel! When we learn that his mum bought him fake Nike runners, it certainly struck a chord with me. It's really hard to keep up with the latest fashion trends and there is a lot of pressure on kids. I instantly felt for Ambrose with his 'Ike' runners and his food allergy. The last line of the extract was kind of funny but dark: the idea that they would mention his knock-off Nike runners in his obituary – Poor Ambrose!

Dara: I really liked how immediately we were brought into the story. The opening line of the extract, 'The day I almost died', was instantly attention grabbing and I was eager to know what would happen to Ambrose. I knew the bullies would do something but the peanut trick was particularly nasty!

Max: I love reading stories written in the first person, as I really get a sense of who Ambrose is based on his words. I love the word games at the start of the extract – I'm better at words than numbers and like doing crosswords and wordsearches. Even the fact that Ambrose calls himself a 'word nerd' makes it pretty clear that he struggles to make friends and fit in. I immediately felt a connection with him as a character, and would love to read the rest of this book!

Explain your choice.
_____
_____
_____
_____
_____
_____

How did you feel while reading this extract?
_____
_____
_____
_____
_____

2 >> Collect and Reflect

 REFLECT ON IT

Read the three student reflections on the poem 'Safe Sounds' by Carol Ann Duffy on page 16 of your textbook.

Tick the reflection that you feel best captures your response to the following question: **Can you relate to the poem 'Safe Sounds'?**

Kevin: I can relate to this poem because the familiar sounds of my home make me feel safe. I could understand exactly what the speaker means because I find it comforting and reassuring when I hear the sound of my mum cooking or calling my name.	
Georgia: The imagery really stood out to me and helped me to imagine lots of comforting sounds such as dogs slurping, TV theme tunes and running water. The poet's use of this descriptive poetic technique helped me to relate to the poem.	
Orlando: Onomatopoeia is one of my favourite poetic devices so far because the sound of the word reflects its meaning. I love this technique in 'Safe Sounds' because I could relate to the sounds and could clearly hear the 'pop' of a bottle. I found it entertaining to practise reading these parts out loud.	

Explain your choice.

_____
_____
_____
_____
_____
_____
_____
_____

How did you feel while reading this poem?

_____
_____
_____
_____
_____
_____
_____

Louder than Words >> Learning Log

GET CREATIVE

Write a review of a film you have seen recently. The film you choose can be old or new. Share your honest opinion, positive and negative, about the film.

or

Imagine you have recently been to a drive-in cinema to see your all-time favourite film. Write a review of the whole experience.

Title: _____

Director: _____

Starring:
_____
_____

Release date: _____

Age rating: _____

Overview: _____
_____
_____
_____
_____
_____
_____
_____
_____
_____
_____
_____

Star rating: ☆ ☆ ☆ ☆ ☆

Recommendation: _____
_____
_____
_____
_____

2 >> Collect and Reflect

 REFLECT ON IT

Read the three student reflections on the review of the film *Luca* on page 20 of your textbook.

Tick the reflection that you feel best captures your response to the following question: **Is this film review well written?**

Kareem: I think this film review is well written. I normally don't like animated films but I think I would like to watch *Luca* since the reviewer calls it a 'little gem'. He is very positive about the film and gave it four and a half stars out of five which is a really good review.	
Jessica: The review is well written but it lacks some consideration for viewers my age. I don't think I would like this film and I'm not really interested in watching it. I think the reviewer is just considering an audience made up of children and adults but forgets about teenagers like me. I will consider all age-groups when making recommendations in my own reviews.	
Alex: This film review provides lots of information and it is structured in a well-organised way. I think it is extremely well-written. The reviewer includes essential and helpful information such as the name of the director, an overview of the plot and a recommendation. This has helped me to work out how to write my own reviews.	

Explain your choice.

_____
_____
_____
_____
_____
_____

Based on the description of the film *Luca* in the review, how interested are you in seeing it?

Interested ☐

Not really interested ☐

Not at all interested ☐

Explain your choice.

_____
_____
_____
_____
_____
_____

Louder than Words >> Learning Log

 GET CREATIVE

Write an open letter to all First Years in which you offer advice on starting a new school. You can include challenges of fitting in and tips for making new friends, for example.

2 >> Collect and Reflect

 REFLECT ON IT

Read the three student reflections on the extract from the play *Holloway Jones* by Evan Placey on page 27 of your textbook.

Tick the reflection that you feel best captures your response to the following question: **What did you think of Holloway's relationships with others in this scene?**

Annie: I could instantly relate to how defensive Holloway is. I think she has difficulty forming relationships and her response to one of the riders, 'Old enough to be your mama', clearly shows that has learnt her putdowns from sitcoms or films. I don't blame her for her response, as the fact that her mom is in jail is obviously a sore point for Holloway and she uses this defence mechanism as a form of protection.

Jason: I love Holloway, her fiery personality really drew me into the scene. I am taken back by how impulsive she is and I felt myself really rooting for her. I don't think violence was the right solution here but I really admire that she wasn't prepared to back down even though there was a group of riders against her.

Martha: I felt particularly moved by Holloway's relationship with the coach. I thought the stage direction for both characters to laugh was a really touching moment and it impacted upon me. Their relationship seems really solid and they appear to have a great understanding of one another. I found myself thinking about the adults in my life who look out for me and could instantly relate to this piece.

Explain your choice.

_____
_____
_____
_____
_____
_____
_____
_____
_____
_____
_____
_____

Louder than Words >> Learning Log

GET CREATIVE

Write about an environment in which you have felt or feel safe. This can take the form of a diary entry or a poem.

or

Prepare a short oral presentation (approx. 2 minutes) in which you review one of the following:
- The last book you read
- A live performance you attended

Rough work

2 » Collect and Reflect

REFLECT ON IT

Reflect on your chosen task by answering the following questions.

I chose this task because …

Explain how two features of your writing are typical of either a diary entry or a poem.

What did you enjoy about doing this task?	What did you find most difficult about the task?

What would you do differently next time?

REFLECT ON IT

Reflect on **Unit 1: Safe Spaces** by answering the following questions.

What do you think the message was in this unit?

What did you enjoy most about this unit?	What did you find most challenging about the unit?

Can you think of any other texts that would work well in this unit?

UNIT 2 Consideration and Compassion

⚡ GET CREATIVE

Write a personal essay based on an act of kindness you saw being done towards someone less fortunate.

2 » Collect and Reflect

REFLECT ON IT

Read the three student reflections on the extract from *OK, Let's Do Your Stupid Idea* by Patrick Freyne on page 33 of your textbook.

Tick the reflection that you feel best captures your response to the following question: **What did you enjoy or dislike about this personal essay?**

Rowan: I really liked how honest and personal the essay was. It's not a story, with characters and plot twists, it's something that happened to the author during his work that stayed with him. I found this really nice as it makes the writer more human and relatable. He found himself getting emotional seeing how the dog reacted to the homeless man. This is a really touching image. I also have a dog who always cheers me up when I'm low and loves to just sit beside me for comfort. In the scene described, I think the man and the dog are getting support from each other!

Aoibheann: I found the writer to be very funny. I loved the line where he said that one of the homeless people at the shelter called him 'Fat Jesus'! It is nice that he doesn't make the piece all about himself and his experience, he makes fun of himself which is very endearing. He also brings some comic relief into a very sad and dark situation.

Scott: I found this piece a little boring, as nothing really happens in it. The writer tells a short anecdote about something that happened to him and he talks about his own feelings, but there's no excitement or tension! I prefer short stories or thrillers that make you constantly wonder what will happen next.

Explain your choice.

_____
_____
_____
_____
_____
_____

What details of this personal essay stayed with you and why?

_____
_____
_____
_____
_____
_____

Louder than Words » Learning Log

REFLECT ON IT

Read the three student reflections on the use of sound in the radio drama *Belong* by Fred O'Connor and Daithí McMahon on page 40 of your textbook.

Tick the student reflection that you most agree with.

Dave: The inclusion of sound effects really adds to the drama of this piece. It helps me to visualise what is happening more clearly. The sound effects of the Luas make the piece really relatable for me.	
Sean: For me, the variety of voices really engages me as a listener. The varying tones of voice captures the atmosphere by allowing me to understand how each character is feeling. The exasperation in Christy's voice really makes me empathise with the hardships he has faced.	
Eithne: The use of the eerie background music to indicate the flashbacks to the past really adds to this radio drama. It helps clarify when we are in the present and when we are revisiting the past, so I wasn't confused.	

Explain your choice.

_____
_____
_____
_____
_____
_____
_____
_____
_____
_____
_____
_____
_____
_____
_____
_____

2 >> **Collect and Reflect**

 GET CREATIVE

Write an article for your school website on the importance of consideration and compassion for all those in our school community.

or

Research the current homeless figures in Ireland. What is the government doing to tackle the issue of homelessness in Ireland? Present your findings to the class.

Rough work

Louder than Words >> Learning Log

REFLECT ON IT

Reflect on your chosen task by answering the following questions.

I chose this task because …
(Article only) Explain how two features of your writing are typical of an article.

What did you enjoy about doing this task?	What did you find most difficult about the task?

What would you do differently next time?

REFLECT ON IT

Reflect on **Unit 2: Consideration and Compassion** by answering the following questions.

What do you think the message was in this unit?

What did you enjoy most about this unit?	What did you find most challenging about the unit?

Can you think of any other texts that would work well in this unit?

2 >> Collect and Reflect

UNIT 3 Sense and Sustainability

 GET CREATIVE

Choose one of the following scenarios and write an email to your teacher.
- You would like to join an afterschool club
- You would like to put yourself forward for the environment committee
- You did not complete your written assignment

| To: |
| From: |
| Subject: |

Louder than Words >> Learning Log

GET CREATIVE

Draw a storyboard tracing the events in *The New Friday*.

1. List the main events or key moments in the play.
2. Draw each part of the scene in the spaces provided.
3. Use the lines to briefly explain what happens in each part.

2 >> Collect and Reflect

 GET CREATIVE

Write a speech encouraging your classmates to take action against climate change. You may like to use one fact or statistic from Greta Thunberg's speech at the UN Climate Action Summit on page 69 of your textbook. Use the following guide to help you.

Opening
- Welcome your audience
- Introduce yourself and your message

_____

First way your classmates can take action against climate change
- Keep your message clear
- Address your audience
- Include a fact or statistic

_____

Louder than Words >> Learning Log

Second way your classmates can take action against climate change
- Keep your message clear
- Address your audience
- Use a rhetorical question

Third way your classmates can take action against climate change
- Keep your message clear
- Address your audience
- Use repetition

Closing
- Use inclusive language
- Thank your audience

2 » Collect and Reflect

REFLECT ON IT

Read the three student reflections on Greta Thunberg's speech at the UN Climate Action Summit on page 69 of your textbook.

Tick the reflection that you feel best captures your response to the following question: **In your opinion, is Greta Thunberg's speech effective?**

Julie: I think that Greta Thunberg's speech is effective because it is evident that she is demanding change. I think she must have made the leaders who were listening uncomfortable when she told them that they have 'stolen [her] dreams and [her] childhood with [their] empty words'. She does not let them get away with this and repeatedly says 'how dare you!'. I think Greta's anger is understandable and this makes her speech even more powerful.

Sinéad: I think that what makes Greta's speech most effective is her use of facts and statistics because it is always good to provide evidence. However, I found it a bit difficult to know exactly what action Greta wants world leaders to take. I understand that the effects of climate change are having a terrible impact on people's lives but I think Greta could specify how world leaders could address the problem – for example, she should demand that they ban fossil fuels. I think this kind of demand would make Greta's speech even more effective than it is already.

Calum: Greta Thunberg's speech is highly effective because she uses inclusive language to speak on behalf of the younger generations 'who have to live with the consequences' of the climate crisis. She includes many features of effective speech writing, which make the delivery of her speech memorable. It is clear that Greta is passionate about the topic, she states her message clearly, addresses her audience, presents facts and statistics, uses rhetorical questions and repetition to force world leaders to listen and take action.

Explain your choice.
_____
_____
_____

Identify Greta Thunberg's message in this speech.
_____
_____

How clear is Greta Thunberg's message in this speech?
Very clear ☐   Somewhat clear ☐   Not very clear ☐

Explain why you feel this way.
_____
_____
_____

Louder than Words ≫ Learning Log

GET CREATIVE

Write a speech about the impact that humans have on the world around us. You should analyse both positive and negative impacts in your speech.

or

Write an email to the principal of your school. In your email, suggest one way in which your school could take action against climate change.

Rough work

2 >> Collect and Reflect

Louder than Words >> Learning Log

REFLECT ON IT

Reflect on your chosen task by answering the following questions.

I chose this task because ...

Explain how two features of your writing are typical of either a speech or an email.

What did you enjoy about doing this task?	What did you find most difficult about the task?

What would you do differently next time?

REFLECT ON IT

Reflect on **Unit 3: Sense and Sustainability** by answering the following questions.

What do you think the message was in this unit?

What did you enjoy most about this unit?	What did you find most challenging about the unit?

Can you think of any other texts that would work well in this unit?

2 >> Collect and Reflect

UNIT 4 Empower and Engage

⚡ GET CREATIVE

Write a blog post about a topic you care about. Remember to include all the features of a blog post on page 78 of your textbook.

29

Louder than Words >> Learning Log

GET CREATIVE

Plan the setting of your own short story.

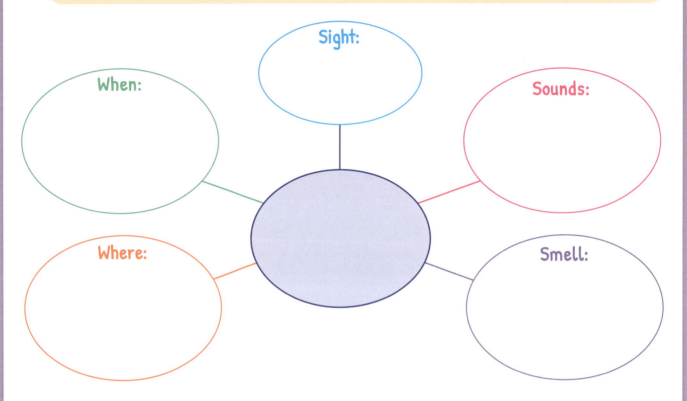

GET CREATIVE

Outline the plot of your short story.

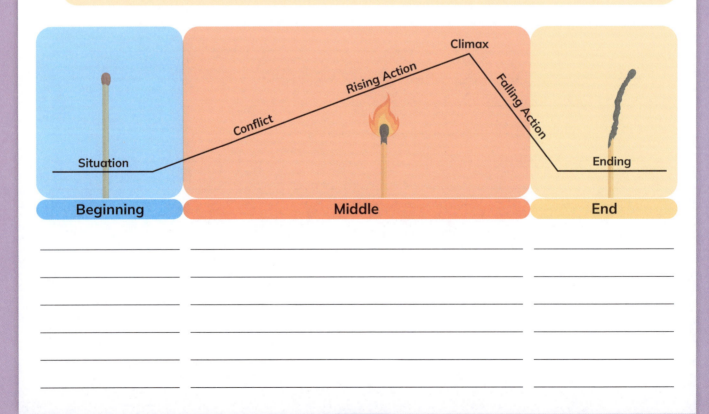

2 » Collect and Reflect

 REFLECT ON IT

Read the three student reflections on the short story 'What if?' by Alyssa McDonald on page 86 of your textbook.

Tick the reflection that you feel best captures your response to the following question: **Did you enjoy reading this short story?**

Anna: I love how we are brought straight into the story. Diana's clenched fists and sweaty palms show the reader how stressed and anxious she is in the classroom setting. I love when stories jump straight into the action and there isn't a long build up!

Mabel: I really liked the dialogue in this story. When Diana says 'um' when she is speaking, it makes it more realistic and natural, just like you would talk normally. The chat she has with the teacher is nice and reassuring, and in the end with a few short words she seems to be making friends. It is great when there is dialogue in stories, it makes them livelier and more interesting, in my opinion.

Lucy: I didn't really enjoy this story. I like stories I can relate to that are about real people and events so I thought it would be easy to connect with since it was about a teenager in class. But I didn't like how the teacher brought up her anxiety, I felt like the girl was put on the spot. Also, chess is a really boring game for old people, I didn't think this part was realistic at all!

Explain your choice.

_____
_____
_____
_____
_____
_____
_____

How did you feel after reading this short story?

_____
_____
_____
_____
_____
_____

Louder than Words >> **Learning Log**

GET CREATIVE

Draw a simple comic that tells a story about a person who overcomes a difficult situation. Give your comic a title.

2 >> Collect and Reflect

 REFLECT ON IT

Read the three student reflections on the advertisement 'All it Takes is Everything' by Three Ireland on page 99 of your textbook.

Tick the reflection that you feel best captures your response to the following question: **What element of this advertisement is the most effective, in your view?**

Justin: I love the special effects in this advertisement. When Johnny Sexton hits the rugby ball and it disintegrates into butterflies it's really effective. I love the fire on Robbie Henshaw to show how hard he is training and how much his muscles are burning. Most of all, as a huge fan of Paul O'Connell, I love how it appears that when he comes up against the rhinoceros he wins. He is such an incredible athlete!	
Maria: The sound and music in this advertisement are the best elements in my view. The voiceover is clearly the great Joe Schmidt, one of the greatest coaches Irish rugby has ever had! The music is really dramatic and tense which helps to build the excitement.	
Sarah: It is great that the hashtag is introduced by the voice over. The repetition of the word 'everything' shows just how important the tournament is and how much preparation has gone into it. The phrase is left resounding in your head long after the ad is finished. This makes the ad memorable and distinct.	

Explain your choice.
_____
_____
_____
_____
_____
_____
_____
_____

How did you feel while watching this advertisement?
_____
_____
_____
_____
_____

Louder than Words >> Learning Log

GET CREATIVE

Your school has decided to set up a podcast and you have been asked to present it. Write the podcast script for the first episode.

Intro (Opening)
_____
_____
_____
_____
_____
_____
_____
_____
_____
_____
_____
_____

Segment 1
_____
_____
_____
_____
_____
_____
_____
_____
_____
_____
_____
_____
_____
_____

Segment 2

_____
_____
_____
_____
_____
_____
_____
_____
_____
_____
_____
_____

Segment 3

_____
_____
_____
_____
_____
_____
_____
_____

Outro (Ending)

_____
_____
_____
_____
_____
_____
_____

Louder than Words >> Learning Log

GET CREATIVE

Write a profile of an athlete or other well-known person that you know or admire. It should include the following information:

- The name of the person you have chosen
- Their date of birth
- What they are known for
- Any other interesting information about the person
- A quote from the person

Name: _____

Date of birth: _____

Known for:
_____
_____
_____
_____

About:
_____
_____
_____
_____
_____
_____
_____
_____
_____
_____
_____
_____
_____
_____

2 >> Collect and Reflect

GET CREATIVE

Write a short story featuring a teenager who struggles to feel confident until something happens to make them see things differently. In your story you should do the following:

- Describe the setting in detail.
- Include a dramatic moment or crisis.
- Show a change in your central character.

or

Write and perform a poem about what it means to be beautiful. Choose to share your performance live in front of your classmates or by making a recording of yourself bringing the poem to life.

Rough work

Louder than Words >> Learning Log

2 >> Collect and Reflect

REFLECT ON IT

Reflect on your chosen task by answering the following questions.

I chose this task because …

Explain how two features of your writing are typical of either a short story or a spoken word poem.

What did you enjoy about doing this task?	What did you find most difficult about the task?

What would you do differently next time?

REFLECT ON IT

Reflect on **Unit 4: Empower and Engage** by answering the following questions.

What do you think the message was in this unit?

What did you enjoy most about this unit?	What did you find most challenging about the unit?

Can you think of any other texts that would work well in this unit?

39

Louder than Words >> Learning Log

UNIT 5 Fast Forward

 GET CREATIVE

Write a letter to someone close to you. Give each of the following bullet points its own paragraph.

- Tell them about your last term in school.
- Fill them in about what you did during the last school break.
- Inform them about what is happening in your personal life at the minute.

Don't forget to frame your letter with a greeting and sign-off.

Louder than Words >> Learning Log

REFLECT ON IT

Read the three student reflections on the extract from *Only Ever Yours* by Louise O'Neill on page 131 of your textbook.

Tick the reflection that you feel best captures your response to the following question: **Do you agree that Louise O'Neill creates a frightening world for her readers in this story?**

Rhys: I would definitely describe the world that the author creates in *Only Ever Yours* as frightening. I was disturbed by the way the narrator describes the world that she inhabits. It sounds like a horrible version of the future, where all hope is lost and everything outside is 'dead'. This idea really scares me.

Samina: I think that Louise O'Neill pays close attention to detail, imagining a terrifying future. She describes how the seas are 'drowning the doomed low-lying countries, never to be seen again' and this is truly frightening. In this world, there are no signs of beauty in nature. There are no animals or trees. I agree wholeheartedly that readers like me must feel utterly terrified reading about a world that is beyond repair.

Tara: I think that there are some signs of hope in the world that Louise O'Neill has created. While the world of *Only Ever Yours* is alarming, I am reminded of the fact that people are still alive. The narrator is a living person who is receiving an education and has the ability to think for herself. She questions what she has been shown. This suggests that there might be the chance for someone to make a difference. I would be frightened to live in the place described but I really hope that the narrator can make a difference somehow.

Explain your choice.

_____
_____
_____
_____
_____
_____

Did this extract make you want to read the novel? Explain your answer.

_____
_____
_____
_____
_____

2 » Collect and Reflect

REFLECT ON IT

Read the three student reflections on the infographic 'A Quick Guide to Artificial Intelligence' on page 134 of your textbook.

Tick the reflection that you feel best captures your response to the following question: **Do you think this infographic is effective?**

Jenny: Infographics are supposed to be really visually eye catching, but this one seemed to have a lot of text. I didn't really like the images – the computer screen and the robots just seemed kind of obvious. I would have liked to see something more futuristic and exciting!

Laura: I really had no clue about artificial intelligence before I looked at this infographic. It is really informative and the three different types are well distinguished from each other.

Anthony: I found the examples really helpful to better understand each type of artificial intelligence. For example, in the Super AI category it says that this kind of AI only exists in science-fiction. It is easier to understand which types of technology exist in the world and which are still limited to our imagination. I also liked the examples at the start, especially 'AI can be in robots that look like people or animals'. Simplifying these definitions makes it much more effective as an infographic.

Explain your choice.

Louder than Words >> Learning Log

REFLECT ON IT

Read the three student reflections on the extract from *Nothing is the End of the World (except the end of the world)* by Bekah Brunstetter on page 137 of your textbook.

Tick the reflection that you feel best captures your response to the following question: **What did you think of the characters Godfrey and Olive?**

Freddie: Godfrey and Olive's words read like a rehearsed script, which adds to their robotic nature. I thought the image that went with the story really highlighted this! I really like the accompanying image on page 137 – the two characters look like emojis, which works really well as they are supposed to be AI students who are trying to act like normal teenagers.	
Jack: Godfrey and Olive really gave me the creeps! It is so weird how they are trying to say all the right things, and behave like teenagers, but by trying so hard they really fail to fit in! They sound more like robots the more they try!	
Caoimhe: Sometimes I wonder if there aren't a few AI students in my own school – some seem to know everything! I thought the points made about Godfrey and Olive by the other students were really interesting – such as how fair is it for normal people to compete with artificial intelligence in different fields? It certainly made me think! I really enjoyed this extract as I love science-fiction and alternative realities.	

Explain your choice.

_____
_____
_____
_____
_____
_____
_____

Based on this extract, would you like to see a performance of this play?

_____
_____
_____
_____
_____
_____
_____

2 >> Collect and Reflect

GET CREATIVE

Practise drawing the following symbols.

LGBTQ+ Pride

Transgender Pride

Flag for the Rights of Persons with Disabilities

Black Lives Matter

Gender Equality

Louder than Words >> Learning Log

GET CREATIVE

Think about your favourite character in a film or novel. Write a description of what you would like to happen to this character in the future.

- Introduce your selected character.
- Briefly explain what happens to this character in the film or novel.
- Explain what you would like to happen to them in the future.

or

Write and perform a dialogue between a teenager today and a teenager in 100 years' time, discussing how the world has changed. Some areas you may consider include:

- the environment
- technology
- equality.

Rough work

2 >> Collect and Reflect

REFLECT ON IT

Reflect on your chosen task by answering the following questions.

I chose this task because …
(Dialogue only) Explain how two features of your writing are typical of dialogue.

What did you enjoy about doing this task?	What did you find most difficult about the task?

What would you do differently next time?

REFLECT ON IT

Reflect on **Unit 5: Fast Forward** by answering the following questions.

What do you think the message was in this unit?

What did you enjoy most about this unit?	What did you find most challenging about the unit?

Can you think of any other texts that would work well in this unit?

Louder than Words >> Learning Log

UNIT 6 Courageous Creativity

REFLECT ON IT

Reflect on the poem 'Introduction to Poetry' by Billy Collins on page 166 of your textbook. The following prompts may help you:

- This poem made me think about …
- One line that stood out to me is …
- One image that has stayed with me is …
- I could imagine how the speaker felt when …
- This reminded me of …
- After I read it, I wondered …
- The reason I would recommend this poem to someone else is …

2 » Collect and Reflect

REFLECT ON IT

Reflect on the poem 'The Starry Night' by Anne Sexton on page 173 of your textbook. The following prompts may help you:

- This poem made me think about …
- One line that stood out to me is …
- One image that has stayed with me is …
- I could imagine how the speaker felt when …
- This reminded me of …
- After I read it, I wondered …
- The reason I would recommend this poem to someone else is …

Louder than Words >> Learning Log

GET CREATIVE

Internal Features		External Features
Marble columns	No roof	Oak beams
Stage balcony	Central yard	Lime-plaster walls
Trapdoor	Galleries	Thatched roof
The Heavens		Flags

Internal

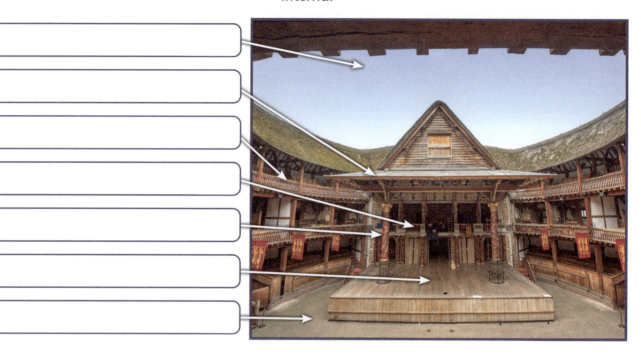

External

GET CREATIVE

Imagine you are a reporter working for a London newspaper in 1599. The Globe Theatre has just opened and there is a buzz of excitement across the city. You have been asked to write a newspaper article about the opening of the Globe Theatre.

THE OLD NEWS

1599

Louder than Words >> Learning Log

GET CREATIVE

Imagine Maria and the others were playing this trick on Malvolio in the present day. Rewrite the scene from *Twelfth Night* using modern language. Remember to include:

- the characters' names on the left
- dialogue on the right
- stage directions in brackets

2 >> Collect and Reflect

Louder than Words >> Learning Log

REFLECT ON IT

Reflect on the extract from *Twelfth Night* by William Shakespeare on page 184 of your textbook. The following prompts may help you:

- This scene made me think about …
- This reminded me of …
- The one line of dialogue that stood out to me is …
- One character that stood out to me is …
- I could imagine performance details such as …
- After I read it, I wondered …
- The reason I would like to read on from this extract is …

REFLECT ON IT

Reflect on the poem 'A Wish' by Nikita Gill on page 190 of your textbook. The following prompts may help you:

- This poem made me think about …
- This poem reminded me of …
- One line that stood out to me is …
- One image that has stayed with me is …
- The most effective poetic device in the poem is …
- After I read the poem, I wondered …
- The reason I would like to read more poems by Nikita Gill is …

Louder than Words >> Learning Log

GET CREATIVE

Write a short poem designed to be shared on social media, inspired by the following painting by L. S. Lowry.

or

Prepare a short oral presentation about what the arts mean to you.

Rough work

2 » Collect and Reflect

REFLECT ON IT

Reflect on your chosen task by answering the following questions.

I chose this task because …

(Poem only) Explain how two features of your writing are typical of a poem.

What did you enjoy about doing this task?	What did you find most difficult about the task?

What would you do differently next time?

Tick the box if you are considering including this piece in your collection of texts for CBA 2 ☐

REFLECT ON IT

Reflect on **Unit 6: Courageous Creativity** by answering the following questions.

What do you think the message was in this unit?

What did you enjoy most about this unit?	What did you find most challenging about the unit?

Can you think of any other texts that would work well in this unit?

Louder than Words >> Learning Log

UNIT 7 Influence and Inform

 GET CREATIVE

Select one of the book covers on page 197 of your textbook and write the blurb you imagine would appear on its back cover.

GET CREATIVE

You have been asked to write a short biography about your favourite person for *TIME* magazine. Include some details of their life, achievements and why they are an inspiration to you and others.

Louder than Words >> Learning Log

 GET CREATIVE

Create a profile of a character from your studied play or novel.

Name of text	
Name of author	
Name of character	
Words to describe this character	
Key relationships	Relationship 1: Relationship 2: Relationship 3:
Important quotes	
The most important thing that happens to this character is …	
Reasons I like/dislike this character	

2 >> Collect and Reflect

REFLECT ON IT

Reflect on the extract from *How To Be Famous* by Caitlin Moran on page 212 of your textbook. The following prompts may help you:

- This extract made me think about …
- The way it was written made me think of …
- One image that has stayed with me is …
- I could imagine how the speaker felt when …
- This reminded me of …
- After I read it, I wondered …
- The reason I would like to read on from this extract is …

Louder than Words >> Learning Log

REFLECT ON IT

Reflect on the poem 'A Life of Influence' by Brian Bilston on page 231 of your textbook. The following prompts may help you:

- This poem made me think about …
- This poem reminded me of …
- One line that stood out to me is …
- One image that has stayed with me is …
- The most effective poetic devices in the poem are …
- I could imagine how the speaker felt when …
- After I read the poem, I wondered …
- The reason I would recommend this poem to someone else is …

GET CREATIVE

Write a debate speech either proposing or opposing the debate motion 'This house believes that attendance at book clubs should be mandatory for all students'.

or

In pairs, write a list of interview questions that you could ask one another in an interview about being a teenager in Ireland in the present day. Take turns conducting your interviews out loud for the rest of the class.

Rough work

Louder than Words >> **Learning Log**

2 » Collect and Reflect

REFLECT ON IT

Reflect on your chosen task by answering the following questions.

I chose this task because …

(Debate speech only) Explain how two features of your writing are typical of a debate speech.

What did you enjoy about doing this task?	What did you find most difficult about the task?

What would you do differently next time?

Tick the box if you are considering including this piece in your collection of texts for CBA 2 ☐

REFLECT ON IT

Reflect on **Unit 7: Influence and Inform** by answering the following questions.

What do you think the message was in this unit?

What did you enjoy most about this unit?	What did you find most challenging about the unit?

Can you think of any other texts that would work well in this unit?

Louder than Words >> Learning Log

UNIT 8 Truth and Trust

REFLECT ON IT

Reflect on the illustration 'You Don't Know What's Going on in People's Lives' by Hazel Mead on page 236 of your textbook. The following prompts may help you:

- This illustration made me think about …
- This reminded me of …
- One character depicted in the image that stood out to me is …
- The drawing style really appealed to me because …
- I like the use of colour in the illustration because …
- After I examined the illustration, I wondered …
- The reason I would like to see more illustrations by Hazel Mead is …

GET CREATIVE

Write about a time in your own life when you or someone close to you told a lie. What happened?

Louder than Words » Learning Log

REFLECT ON IT

Reflect on the short play *Fault* by Ann Cartwright on page 248 of your textbook. The following prompts may help you:

- This short play made me think about …
- This reminded me of …
- The one line of dialogue that stood out to me is …
- One character that stood out to me is …
- I could imagine performance details such as …
- After I read it, I wondered …

2 >> Collect and Reflect

GET CREATIVE

Write the monologue that Sammy might deliver on the same night as Leah in *Bird*.

Louder than Words >> Learning Log

REFLECT ON IT

Reflect on the extract from *We Were Liars* by E. Lockhart on page 262 of your textbook. The following prompts may help you:

- This extract made me think about …
- The way it was written made me think of …
- One image that has stayed with me is …
- I could imagine how the speaker felt when …
- This reminded me of …
- After I read it, I wondered …
- The reason I would like to read on from this extract is …

GET CREATIVE

Write an article for your school magazine on the importance of freedom of expression in literature.

or

Script and read aloud a monologue that you imagine a central character from one of your studied texts would deliver at a crucial moment in the plot.

Rough work

Louder than Words >> Learning Log

REFLECT ON IT

Reflect on your chosen task by answering the following questions.

I chose this task because ...

Explain how two features of your writing are typical of an article or a monologue.

What did you enjoy about doing this task?	What did you find most difficult about the task?

What would you do differently next time?

Tick the box if you are considering including this piece in your collection of texts for CBA 2 ☐

REFLECT ON IT

Reflect on **Unit 8: Truth and Trust** by answering the following questions.

What do you think the message was in this unit?

What did you enjoy most about this unit?	What did you find most challenging about the unit?

Can you think of any other texts that would work well in this unit?

UNIT 9 Animated Adventures

REFLECT ON IT

Reflect on the extract from *Northern Lights – The Graphic Novel* by Philip Pullman on page 291 of your textbook. The following prompts may help you:

- This extract made me think about …
- I liked the use of colour because …
- One visual image that has stayed with me is …
- The graphics appealed to me because …
- This reminded me of …
- After I read it, I wondered …
- The reason I would like to read more graphic novels like this is …

Louder than Words >> Learning Log

GET CREATIVE

Design your own comic or *manga* on the theme of 'truth'.

REFLECT ON IT

Reflect on the extract from *The Arrival* by Shaun Tan on page 307 of your textbook. The following prompts may help you:

- This extract made me think about …
- This reminded me of …
- The style of illustration stood out to me because …
- The use of black and white is effective because …
- Because there are no words in the book …
- One character depicted in the images who stood out to me is …
- One image that has stayed with me is …
- After I read it, I wondered …
- The reason I would like to read the rest of *The Arrival* is …

Louder than Words >> Learning Log

GET CREATIVE

Create your own visual narrative based on a novel you have studied in English class. Choose an important moment in the novel and create a comic strip to represent what happens.

or

You are proposing a graphic story to your book club as its next read. Choose either a comic, graphic novel, *manga* or silent book (you may use an example from this unit) and give a short presentation to explain why you think it would be a good suggestion for the club.

Rough work

2 >> Collect and Reflect

Louder than Words » Learning Log

REFLECT ON IT

Reflect on your chosen task by answering the following questions.

I chose this task because …

(Comic only) Explain how two features of your writing are typical of graphic storytelling.

What did you enjoy about doing this task?	What did you find most difficult about the task?

What would you do differently next time?

Tick the box if you are considering including this piece in your collection of texts for CBA 2 ☐

REFLECT ON IT

Reflect on **Unit 9: Animated Adventures** by answering the following questions.

What do you think the message was in this unit?

What did you enjoy most about this unit?	What did you find most challenging about the unit?

Can you think of any other texts that would work well in this unit?

UNIT 10 Individuals and Identities

REFLECT ON IT

Reflect on the article 'That's Not My Name' by Ola Majekodunmi on page 339 of your textbook. The following prompts may help you:

- This article made me think about …
- This reminded me of …
- By reading the experience of someone who is affected by this issue, I learned …
- I can imagine how the writer felt when …
- One thing that has stayed with me is …
- After I read the article, I wondered …
- The reason I would like to learn more about this issue is …

Louder than Words >> Learning Log

GET CREATIVE

Fill in the gaps in the song 'Anseo' by Denise Chaila with your own words to create a new version of the song.

If you're looking for your _____:
Anseo
_____:
Anseo
_____:
C'est moi
I am not a _____ I'm a _____, sha

Call _____
Someone call the BBC
Everything's feeling _____
But don't watch, I'll give you sum'n to see
Keep your _____
I am not afraid of _____
Can't touch my _____

My little brother could _____
With two good minutes and a lickle Google search
Realise that I'm _____, but I'll _____
Don't sleep on me _____,

I don't lack in _____
Even my vices can't hold me back
I've done all the _____
All the sound checks
Vision is high res

I'm not inclined
To stop now that I've started
Back track, side step or half heart it
Couldn't predict this _____
Can't navigate my stars
And no one can _____

2 » Collect and Reflect

REFLECT ON IT

Reflect on the extract from *Pronoun* by Evan Placey on page 364 of your textbook. The following prompts may help you:

- After I read the extract, I felt …
- This made me think about …
- The one thing that really struck me was …
- When I finished reading the extract, I thought …
- What I would like to know more about is …

Louder than Words >> Learning Log

GET CREATIVE

Write a personal essay with the title 'Me, Myself and I'.

or

Create the script for a radio documentary on the subject of the importance of being yourself. Record your documentary and share it with the class.

Rough work

2 >> Collect and Reflect

Louder than Words >> Learning Log

REFLECT ON IT

Reflect on your chosen task by answering the following questions.

I chose this task because ...

Explain how two features of your writing are typical of either a personal essay or a radio documentary script.

What did you enjoy about doing this task?	What did you find most difficult about the task?

What would you do differently next time?

Tick the box if you are considering including this piece in your collection of texts for CBA 2 ☐

REFLECT ON IT

Reflect on **Unit 10: Individuals and Identities** by answering the following questions.

What do you think the message was in this unit?

What did you enjoy most about this unit?	What did you find most challenging about the unit?

Can you think of any other texts that would work well in this unit?

UNIT 11 Power and Powerlessness

GET CREATIVE

One of your studied novels or plays is being adapted into a musical. Select a key moment from a play or novel that you have studied and work with a partner to write song lyrics describing the moment that you have selected.

Louder than Words >> Learning Log

REFLECT ON IT

Reflect on the poem 'Invictus' by William Ernest Henley on page 394 of your textbook. The following prompts may help you:

- This poem made me think about …
- This poem reminded me of …
- One line that stood out to me is …
- One image that has stayed with me is …
- The most effective poetic devices in the poem are …
- I could imagine how the speaker felt when …
- After I read the poem, I wondered …
- The reason I would recommend this poem to someone else is …

2 » Collect and Reflect

REFLECT ON IT

Reflect on the poem 'Standing' by Carol Kinane on page 397 of your textbook. The following prompts may help you:

- This poem made me think about …
- This poem reminded me of …
- One line that stood out to me is …
- One image that has stayed with me is …
- The most effective poetic devices in the poem are …
- I could imagine how the speaker felt when …
- After I read the poem, I wondered …
- The reason I would recommend this poem to someone else is …

Louder than Words >> Learning Log

REFLECT ON IT

Reflect on the extract from *When Hitler Stole Pink Rabbit* by Judith Kerr on page 400 of your textbook. The following prompts may help you:

- This extract made me think about …
- The way it was written made me think of …
- One image that has stayed with me is …
- This reminded me of …
- After I read it, I wondered …
- The reason I would like to read on from this extract is …

GET CREATIVE

Write an epilogue to add to the end of the Shakespeare play you have studied.

Think about the following:
- Which character will you select to deliver the lines?
- What aspect of the play will the epilogue reflect back on?

Louder than Words >> Learning Log

GET CREATIVE

Write a comparison of two characters from texts you have studied – one who abuses their power and one who uses their power for good.

or

Prepare a scene of a play in which one character has power over another character or characters.

- When you have written your script, work in a pair or group to perform or record your scene.
- You may wish to include other elements of performance or production to bring your scene to life, such as props or sound effects.

Louder than Words >> Learning Log

REFLECT ON IT

Reflect on your chosen task by answering the following questions.

I chose this task because …

Explain how two features of your writing are typical of either a comparison or a scene from a play.

What did you enjoy about doing this task?	What did you find most difficult about the task?

What would you do differently next time?

Tick the box if you are considering including this piece in your collection of texts for CBA 2 ☐

REFLECT ON IT

Reflect on **Unit 11: Power and Powerlessness** by answering the following questions.

What do you think the message was in this unit?

What did you enjoy most about this unit?	What did you find most challenging about the unit?

Can you think of any other texts that would work well in this unit?

UNIT 12 Stand Up, Speak Out!

GET CREATIVE

The novel *Moxie* has been made into a film. Choose a novel you have read that has been adapted into a film that you have watched and compare the two texts.

Name of text(s):	
Author	Director
Best moment in the novel:	Best moment in the film:
Strengths of the novel:	Strengths of the film:
Weaknesses of the novel:	Weaknesses of the film:
Opening scene/chapter: Which do you prefer and why?	
Closing scene/chapter: Which do you prefer and why?	

Louder than Words >> Learning Log

 REFLECT ON IT

Reflect on the extract from *Moxie* by Jennifer Mathieu on page 419 of your textbook. The following prompts may help you:

- This extract made me think about …
- The way it was written made me think of …
- One image that has stayed with me is …
- This reminded me of …
- After I read it, I wondered …
- The reason I would like to read on from this extract is …

2 » Collect and Reflect

 GET CREATIVE

Choose a scene from one of your studied texts and write it as a screenplay. Remember to include the features of a screenplay on page 427 of your textbook.

Name of text: _____

Author: _____

Louder than Words >> Learning Log

2 » Collect and Reflect

REFLECT ON IT

Reflect on the video *A Short History of Irish Travellers* by Cork Traveller Women's Network on page 438 of your textbook. The following prompts may help you:

- This video made me think about …
- The style of animation appealed to me because …
- One fact that has stayed with me is …
- This reminded me of …
- After I watched it, I wondered …

Louder than Words >> Learning Log

GET CREATIVE

Carry out an interview with someone, either real or imaginary, who you feel has fought for change in a positive way.

or

Write an article for your school website in which you campaign to change something you feel passionate about in your own school.

Rough work

Louder than Words » Learning Log

REFLECT ON IT

Reflect on your chosen task by answering the following questions.

I chose this task because …

Explain how two features of your writing are typical of either an interview or an article.

What did you enjoy about doing this task?	What did you find most difficult about the task?

What would you do differently next time?

Tick the box if you are considering including this piece in your collection of texts for CBA 2 ☐

REFLECT ON IT

Reflect on **Unit 12: Stand Up, Speak Out!** by answering the following questions.

What do you think the message was in this unit?

What did you enjoy most about this unit?	What did you find most challenging about the unit?

Can you think of any other texts that would work well in this unit?

3 Fire Ahead with Assessment

The skills you learn during your Junior Cycle English course are assessed in the following ways:

- Two Classroom-based Assessments, which you will prepare for and complete during lesson time:
  - **CBA 1: Oral Communication** in Second Year
  - **CBA 2: Collection of the Student's Texts** in Third Year
- An **Assessment Task** following CBA 2, which is worth 10% of your final mark in English
- A **Final Assessment** in the form of a written exam at the end of Third Year

In this section you will find out more about these forms of assessment and find advice on how to prepare for and tackle each one.

CBA 1: Oral Communication

CBA 1 examines your oral communication skills in the form of an individual or group presentation or other method of communication. Your oral communication should be approximately three minutes long.

Completing CBA 1

Step 1. Select your topic

A good place to start is to decide on a topic. This could be a person you are interested in, a hobby, an organisation or something you would like to research. Knowing what you want to speak about or present on will give you a focus for your research.

When choosing a topic, think about the following questions:
- Have you read any interesting novels or graphic novels or seen any good films recently?
- Have you read or seen any interesting plays recently?
- Do you enjoy reciting or writing poetry?
- Have you read any interesting biographies or autobiographies recently?
- Is there a story that has been in the news recently that you would like to know more about?
- Do you have any unusual or special skills?
- Do you have a favourite hobby or sport that your classmates might be interested to find out about?
- Are you curious about the habits and behaviours of your classmates? For example, how many people visit their local library, how many shop online, or which social media platforms are the most common?
- Do you belong to a local community organisation or voluntary group that people would be interested to hear about?

Louder than Words >> **Learning Log**

 CHAT IT OUT

Take turns to ask your partner three of the questions above. Did any good ideas for an oral presentation come up?

The most important thing is to choose a topic you are interested in. You will not be able to deliver your oral presentation confidently and fluently if you do not know what you are talking about! The following table contains some suggestions.

A Famous Person/A Person I Admire	Charities/Community programmes
<ul><li>Greta Thunberg</li><li>Ruth Bader Ginsburg</li><li>Michael D. Higgins</li><li>David Attenborough</li></ul>	<ul><li>St John's Ambulance</li><li>Special Olympics Ireland</li><li>Irish Cancer Society</li><li>RNLI</li><li>Pieta House</li><li>TidyTowns</li></ul>
Popular Culture	**My Favourite sport/My Sporting Hero**
<ul><li>Charli D'Amelio</li><li>Bechdel test</li><li>Social media</li><li>Banksy</li><li>*Manga*</li></ul>	<ul><li>Simone Biles</li><li>Naomi Osaka</li><li>Rory McElroy</li><li>Lewis Hamilton</li><li>Cristiano Ronaldo</li><li>Katie Taylor</li></ul>
History	**Science**
<ul><li>Rosa Parks</li><li>Moon landing</li><li>Hiroshima</li><li>Titanic</li><li>Easter Rising</li><li>Fall of the Berlin Wall</li></ul>	<ul><li>Climate change</li><li>Cloning</li><li>Hubble Space Telescope</li><li>Large Hadron Collider</li><li>Vaccinations</li></ul>
Literature	**Film**
<ul><li>Amanda Gorman</li><li>J. K. Rowling</li><li>Jane Austen</li><li>J. R. R. Tolkien</li><li>Roald Dahl</li></ul>	<ul><li>Marvel series</li><li>*Anime*</li><li>Horror films</li><li>Oscar-winning movies</li><li>My favourite director</li></ul>

CHAT IT OUT

Select a topic from the table below. Start the timer and see if you can talk on that subject for 30 seconds without stopping!

Once you have chosen a topic, think about which of the following oral formats would work best to present it in an interesting way:

Performance	A scripted or improvised performance, including drama, alone or with others
Presentation	Speaking with or without notes or a reading of a prepared script
Interview	Responding to questions asked by the teacher and/or other students. You may take on the role of interviewer as well as interviewee in a dialogue
Response to stimulus material	Stimulus material – e.g. a picture, an article, a song, a book, or anything else – may be used by you or the teacher to start or guide oral communication (the idea is that it 'stimulates' the presentation, or gets you started talking about the topic)

Step 2. Carry out your research

In order to fully inform yourself about a subject, you must research it. This means finding out more about the topic you have chosen by actively seeking out information. Start by thinking which form of research best suits your needs: primary or secondary.

Primary research

Primary research is when you gather information yourself, instead of getting it from other sources. Forms of primary research include:

- inviting someone to share their knowledge or experience by writing letters and sending emails
- carrying out an interview
- carrying out a survey.

For example, if you are researching a topic that relates to your classmates, you might use an interview or survey to find out their opinions.

 To carry out a survey:
1. Make a list of relevant questions: work alone or with a group to decide which questions will help you to gather the required information.
2. Ask the questions: when you have chosen the questions, present them to the group. The group may fill out a paper or online questionnaire.
3. Analyse the results: you may wish to convert figures to percentages in order to present your findings later on.
4. Present your findings: show your results using a table, graph or chart. You may also wish to quote responses to the questions as part of your presentation.

Louder than Words >> Learning Log

Software and apps can help you carry out your research and organise your findings. For example, for surveys or gaining feedback you could use Google Forms, SurveyMonkey or Padlet.

Secondary research

Secondary research is when you get information from other sources. Forms of secondary research include:

- gathering official facts and statistics from organisations or groups
- watching documentaries
- reading information in books
- using the internet to find information.

For example, if you are researching a topic to present to your class, you may find information at the library or on the internet.

To carry out an online search:

- **Use specific search terms**, e.g. 'Causes of the First World War' will be more effective than 'Why did the First World War begin?'
- **Place an asterisk at the end of a word** to search for a variation of that key word, e.g. 'France* First World War' will show variations of the word 'France', such as 'French'
- **Use quotation marks** to search for a phrase rather than individual key words, e.g. "Hitler's rise to power" will show results including this entire phrase
- **Include the word AND** in capital letters to show two search results, e.g. 'Painters AND sculptors' will show results for both key words
- **Include the word OR** in capital letters to show two similar results, e.g. 'Poems OR plays by Shakespeare' will show both options for Shakespeare's works
- **Include the word NOT** in capital letters to filter particular results, e.g. 'J. K. Rowling Books NOT Harry Potter' will show results that do not include the Harry Potter series

MASTER THE LANGUAGE

Look up one of the authors you have studied during your Junior Cycle English course using an online search engine and record the number of results you get. Then search the author again, this time applying one of the methods in the list above.

- How do the numbers of results differ?
- In what ways are the results more focused?

Make sure the information you are gathering is from reliable sources. Use more than one source of information to cross-reference to ensure the details you have found are accurate. If you are unsure if the information from an online source is reliable, search the same information on different sources and see if it matches. Remember that online sources can vary in their reliability.

Reliable sources include:
- **Museum websites:** These organisations are run by experts who want to provide the most accurate information. The website address usually ends in .org
- **RTÉ News:** While no news site is perfect, you can mostly trust that their news is factual
- **University/educational websites:** These are run by professionals/academics who are experts in their subject areas. The website address usually ends in .edu
- **Government websites:** If the website address ends with .gov.ie, you can trust that it is reliable.

The following sources are useful, but you should use them carefully:
- **Other news sites:** Find out about their reputation for objectivity and reliability before you use them as a source.
- **Wikipedia:** This can be a good starting point for getting an overview of a topic but it can be altered, so make sure you combine it with other sources.
- **Blogs:** A blog can be written by anyone, so check who is writing it and judge for yourself if they can be trusted. They may be pushing a specific agenda or viewpoint.
- **Twitter:** Anyone can post on this platform and incorrect information can be shared easily.
- **YouTube:** Check who has posted the video. Is it an organisation (e.g. the History Channel) or an individual?

Step 3. Write up your findings

You will need to write up your notes or accompanying text at this stage, but keep in mind this is not a written assessment – you will be judged on what you say and how you deliver it.

- If you plan to give a presentation (using PowerPoint or Keynote, for example), you can write text to accompany each slide but you should keep text to a minimum (no more than 30 words per slide). Remember that your audience should be listening to you, they should not be expected to read large chunks of text. The visual slides are there to complement what you are saying, not replace it.
- If you are going to give a performance, write out some notes on how to deliver each part, adding in tone and volume, or gestures and expression.
- If you are going to deliver a speech, you will need to carefully plan your speech.

 Revisit page 68 of your textbook to refresh what you know about speeches.

Redraft your work using the following checklist.

All presentations
- ✓ Clear purpose or objective
- ✓ Clear introduction
- ✓ Links from one point to the next
- ✓ Clear conclusion
- ✓ Facts checked
- ✓ Correct length (approx. 3 minutes)

Visual presentations
- ✓ Information matches with visual aids (e.g. slides)
- ✓ Visual aids don't contain too much information
- ✓ Text on visual aids is correct (spelling and grammar)
- ✓ There is clear transition between each slide
- ✓ Looks clear and easy to follow

At this stage you may get some feedback from your teacher. Make any suggested changes and write your final draft.

Step 3. Communicate

Communication is what your research, planning and writing for CBA 1 has been leading to. It is not acceptable to read from a sheet of paper or slides. Rehearse your presentation or performance out loud.

When rehearsing, think about the following questions:
- Am I speaking clearly?
- Am I speaking at the right pace?
- Am I speaking at the right volume?
- Have I used expression and intonation where necessary?
- Have I included interesting persuasive or engaging techniques to keep my audience interested?

Example

Take a look at the following presentation, supported with slides. Note that the slides are simple and only feature key words, while the rest is explained orally.

> Hi everyone! My name is Marian and I am here today to talk about Special Olympics. This topic is particularly close to my heart as I have been volunteering with them for the past three years. My mum has also been a volunteer for years, so that's how I got into it.
>
> According to their website, 'Special Olympics is the world's largest sports organisation for children and adults with intellectual and physical disabilities, providing year-round training and activities to 5 million participants and Unified Sports partners in 172 countries.'

Eunice Kennedy Shriver
- Founded in the 1960s
- Ireland in 1978
- World Games 2003

> In 1963, Eunice Kennedy Shriver, sister of then US President John F. Kennedy, started a day camp called Camp Shriver for children with intellectual and physical difficulties. Her sister Rosemary was born with intellectual difficulties and it is often said that this served as her inspiration for setting up this camp.
>
> The Irish Special Olympics committee was founded in 1978. As the organisation grew, the Irish committee made a bid to host the World Games for the first time outside of the US, and in 2003 the bid was successful.
>
> How many people here volunteer with a local charity or community organisation? In my view, it is these kinds of groups and organisations that communities are built on and that's why, now more than ever, they are so important.

Sports

- Alpine Skiing
- Athletics
- Badminton
- Basketball
- Bocce
- Bowling
- Equestrian
- Floorball
- Football
- Golf
- Gymnastics
- Kayaking
- Pitch & Putt
- Swimming
- Table Tennis
- Motor Activities

> Here is a list of sports that are included in the Special Olympics. There are sports clubs all over the country providing training and opportunities for athletes. Some sports are more popular in Ireland than others.

Benefits

- Inclusion
- Skills
- Community

> Currently almost 8,000 athletes from across Ireland participate in 15 different sports through the Special Olympics.
>
> Through the sports, health and leadership programmes athletes develop physical, mental and emotional skills. They learn new and important skills, get fit and make lots of new friends!
>
> Anyone over the age of 15 can volunteer in Ireland and there are lots of local clubs and organisations across all the different sports.

My Volunteering Experience

Tivoli Tigers Gymnastics Club

I volunteer at a Special Olympics gymnastics club once a week. I am a gymnast myself so I have a special interest in the sport. I work alongside the other coaches teaching skills, playing games and choreographing routines. I really love it, and the athletes are so enthusiastic!

World Games 2003

My mum was a volunteer during the World Games in 2003 when it came to Ireland. She told me all about her experience as a gymnastics official and how much she enjoyed it. It was an incredible event, with the opening and closing ceremonies being held in Croke Park.

After the games a sculpture was built in Dublin Castle with the Special Olympics logo and the 30,000 names of all the volunteers as a thank you – my mum's name is there!

Louder than Words >> Learning Log

> Here is a list of the sources that I used for this project. If anyone has any questions, I would be happy to answer them!

Step 4. Reflect on CBA 1

After you have completed your Oral Communication task you will be asked to reflect on the whole process. To prepare for this, note down your thoughts and plans as you work and think about how you are getting on.

Consider the following:
- How did you come up with your topic?
- What challenges did you face along the way?
- What advice did you get from your peers? Your teacher?
- What helped you to prepare for the task?
- How did you feel before? During preparation? After?

3 >> **Fire Ahead with Assessment**

At the end of the process, you will be given a Student Reflection Note to be completed during class time and submitted to the teacher. Look at the following example based on the presentation above.

SCHOOL St Joseph's College	STUDENT Marian O'Sullivan
TITLE Special Olympics	

The part I played in communication and preparation, including material used/accessed
I started by researching the history and background of the organisation using the official website. I used careful research skills in gathering the right information for my presentation and had to be selective when deciding what was relevant and what wasn't. I also spoke to other volunteers and leaders in my organisation to get their feedback, and from there I had a strong idea of the purpose of my presentation. As well as drawing on my own personal experience, I asked my mum questions about her experience. Once I had completed my research, I made notes and then organised the material into sections. These sections then became the basis for my slides. Once I had created my slides, fact checked them and looked for spelling mistakes, I started practising my presentation out loud. At first, I used notes to help me but the more I practised the more confident I became and I was able to use the key words on the slides as prompts for my speech.

Personal reflection on the Oral Communication	
One important thing I learned from doing the task:	Things I would change or try to improve on:
I learned that careful and accurate research is really important. When trying to establish the year that the organisation was founded, I found different years on different websites. This showed me the importance of verifying my sources. These sources should then be included at the end of my presentation. This shows the audience that the information is accurate and the presentation has been well researched.	I would practise transitioning from slide to slide more. It is difficult to know when to move on to the next slide, for fear that you haven't covered everything in that section. Saying it out loud again and again really helps. I would also try to include more about my personal experience. This seems to be the most interesting aspect for the audience and it means I can speak honestly and personally.

Student Marian O'Sullivan	Teacher Mr Fallon	Date 30 September 2022

CBA 2: Collection of the Student's Texts

CBA 2 examines your writing skills. During Second and Third Year you will be expected to build a collection of texts that will arise from schoolwork. It is recommended that you retain at least four pieces of work across four genres.

Genres may include but are not limited to:

- an opinion piece
- a descriptive piece
- a functional writing piece
- an autobiographical piece
- a critique
- a humorous piece
- a media piece
- a narrative
- a poem
- a film or drama script

 Revisit page 1 of this book to refresh the features and language style of different genres of writing.

The texts you select for assessment will be accompanied by any previous drafts and a Student Reflection Note.

Completing CBA 2

Step 1. Plan and write your first draft

The best way to prepare for CBA 2 is to read lots of different styles of writing – pick up a book, magazine, newspaper and go online to read blogs and watch famous speeches being delivered. These will inspire your own writing. Find a topic that you are interested in or choose something that is topical. Try to imitate the style of these samples of writing when you have your pen in your hand.

Begin by jotting down your initial ideas for your piece, or write a bullet pointed list if you prefer. You should consider the features and language style for the genre you are writing in.

Once you have a clear plan in place, start writing your first draft. Drafting each piece of written work is essential as it allows you to develop your work to its full potential.

Step 2. Review, edit and redraft your work

Reviewing, editing and redrafting your work is part of being an active learner. An active learner thinks about their work, asks questions, listens to feedback, reads through corrections, seeks advice from others and researches how to make their work better.

To review, edit and redraft your work you should:
- Proofread your first draft to ensure that you have made no spelling, grammar or punctuation errors. Use a different-coloured pen to make any changes needed.
- Make sure you have included the correct features of the genre you are writing in. For example, if you are writing an article make sure you include a headline, or if you are writing a diary entry make sure you include the date.
- Reread your work and make a note of any changes you would like to make. For example, could you add more description to draw in your readers?
- Submit your work to your teacher for correction and ask questions about what you could do to improve.
- Ask a peer to read over your work. Listen to their feedback on your work and change any areas that you feel you could improve.
- Read over your piece one last time to ensure that there are no spelling or grammar mistakes and that you are happy with all the changes.

Below is a sample first draft of a task that asked students to 'Prepare a speech that will be delivered to your peers before their exams commence.'

First draft

Good morning.

Today is a very nervous day. it is the day before the exams start. I know what you are all thinking and it's the same for me, nerves, worry and fear. It seems like only yesterday we were all gathered together in this hall for our very first assembly as first years and now here we are gathered together as third year students about to sit our Junior Cycle exam. I want to offer some advice as your class representative. Try to get a good night's sleep tonight and remember to bring a bottle of water with you tomorrow. We have worked so hard over the last three years and we are more prepared for the exams than we feel. Nerves are a normal part of exams so expect to feel those butterflies tomorrow, just remember, we are all in this together. Wishing you all the very best of luck.

Look at the teacher and peer feedback received on the piece.

Teacher feedback
- Don't forget to address your audience at the beginning of the speech.
- Aim to include more features of a speech. I would suggest reading over the features table on page 68 of your textbook – this will help to develop your speech further.
- Use a thesaurus to see if you can improve on one or two descriptive words that you have used in your first draft. This could improve your language skills and expression in the second draft.
- Incorporate paragraphs into your second draft.

- Proofread for punctuation and capital letters, there are areas that require amending.
- Sign off your speech by thanking your classmates for their attention.

Peer feedback

Maybe try to include some humour. The target audience is your classmates, so I think they would relate to something a little more light-hearted and funny.

Now take a look at the second draft of the piece to see how the student took the corrections and changes on board.

Second draft

Good morning, fellow classmates.

Today is a very nerve-racking day for all of us. As you are fully aware, tomorrow marks the beginning of our Junior Cycle exams. It doesn't seem that long ago since we gathered in this hall as First Years for our first ever assembly, now here we are, three years later, embarking on our first ever state exam.

On average, 50,000 students up and down the country sit the Junior Cycle exams every year. Can I ask anyone who is feeling apprehensive to raise their hands? Just as I suspected, we have all raised our hands, which is a reminder that we, along with those thousands of other students, are in this together!

As your class representative, I don't want to repeat the advice you'll have read a hundred times in study guides. Instead, I'd like to remind you of the wise words of Ms Malone, our year head, who says 'cramming for twelve hours on the night before an exam, locked away like a prisoner in a cell won't do for you what a walk, some meditation, a good night's sleep and a few hours of revision will do'. I want to reassure you that Ms Malone is correct. And so, I propose that we meet tomorrow morning, half an hour before the exam starts, to do a 20-minute meditation in the Sport's Hall. Everyone is welcome and I hope to see you there. Let's calm the pre-exam nerves together.

I want to leave you now with a quote from Arnold Schwarzenegger: 'Strength does not come from winning. Your struggles develop your strengths. When you go through hardships and decide not to surrender, that is true strength.' What I take from these words is that persistence and effort are what makes us who we are, not results and awards.

Thank you for giving me your attention and the very best of luck for tomorrow.

Step 3. Reflect on CBA 2

After you have selected your texts for CBA 2, you will be asked to reflect on the whole process. To prepare for this, note down your thoughts and plans as you work and think about how you are getting on.

3 >> **Fire Ahead with Assessment**

Consider the following:
- Why did you choose to write in this particular genre?
- How did you ensure that you were including features from your chosen genre?
- What challenges did you face along the way?
- What advice did you get from your peers or your teacher?
- What helped you to prepare for the task?
- How did you feel before the task, during preparation and afterwards?

At the end of the process, you will be given a Student Reflection Note to be completed during class time and submitted to the teacher. Look at the following example based on the speech above.

SCHOOL Park Lodge Secondary School	STUDENT Max Hughes
TITLE and GENRE Speech to be delivered to your fellow peers offering encouragement before sitting exams	

I chose this genre because ...
I really enjoy speech writing. I think it gives you the opportunity really engage with an audience and motivate your listeners.

My assessment of my work ...	
What I learned from creating this text: I realised the importance of obtaining feedback from my teacher. Once I read over my first draft, I noticed a few punctuation errors that I had made which I was able to identify and correct. However, when I received the first draft back from my teacher, I realised that there were further features of speech writing that I could include. Overall, this process has really helped me to improve on my writing skills. I learned the value of completing a thorough proofread while revising the features of a genre.	What I would do differently next time: First, I would use the checklist of features for my genre to ensure that I have included all the necessary requirements for my piece of writing. This is a really valuable resource that allows me to do an independent check of my work and ensure that the requirements of the genre are fulfilled. Second, I would read my first draft once more before submitting it to my teacher. I don't think reading over my work once was sufficient. I believe if I came back to the speech with fresh eyes after my first set of edits, I would have recognised further areas where I could improve.
Student Max Hughes	Teacher Ms O'Grady — Date 15 March 2022

Assessment Task

In Third Year, you will complete an Assessment Task, which involves reflecting on your writing process during the completion of CBA 2. Your teacher will give you an Assessment Task booklet to be completed in class under exam conditions. This booklet is then sent to the exam board to be marked and is worth 10% of your final grade in English.

The purpose of the Assessment task is to:
- discuss your experience of compiling your Collection of Texts
- reflect on your writing
- evaluate your writing
- demonstrate the skills you have developed

MASTER THE LANGUAGE

When you have completed your Collection of Texts (CBA 2), use the following table to prepare for your Assessment Task.

I have ...	Text 1	Text 2
Given my tasks appropriate titles	Title:	Title:
Identified the genre of my writing samples	Genre:	Genre:
Included the features appropriate to each genre	Features:	Features:
Used language appropriate to each genre/topic	Language style:	Language style:
Made changes to improve my writing	Change: How it improved my writing:	Change: How it improved my writing:

Completing the Assessment Task

Step 1. Discuss and reflect

Before you write in the Assessment Task booklet, you will discuss and reflect on the writing process as a class. During this stage, your teacher may share some stimulus material with you, which you should read, watch or listen to carefully. For example, you might be shown an interview with an author – think about what the author is saying: can you relate to their experience as a writer?

Once you have been shown the stimulus material, you will take part in a discussion about what you have read, watched or listened to. Think about how it relates to your own experience of writing when you were completing CBA 2 and discuss in class.

MASTER THE LANGUAGE

> If I waited for perfection, I would never write a word.
> *Margaret Atwood*

> Most of writing is editing. It is the responsibility of the author to provide the reader with the best material possible.
> *Harry Heckel*

> The first draft is black and white. Editing gives the story colour.
> *Emma Hill*

> An opening line should invite the reader to begin the story. It should say: Listen, come in here. You want to know about this.
> *Stephen King*

1. Reflect on two of the quotes provided in the stimulus material above. Write your response to both statements in the spaces provided.

    In responding to the stimulus material, think about your own experience of writing.

    (a) Consider the editing process. How did you edit, change and improve your writing?

    (b) Consider your use of descriptive writing. How did you bring your writing to life for the reader?

    Quote 1

Louder than Words >> Learning Log

Reflecting on this quote and my own writing:
_____
_____
_____
_____
_____
_____
_____
_____
_____
_____

Quote 2

Reflecting on this quote and my own writing:
_____
_____
_____
_____
_____
_____
_____
_____
_____
_____

Your teacher will then give you the Assessment Task booklet and a set of writing prompts. The booklet is approximately four pages in length. During this time, you will:
- read the questions in Section A
- think about the writing prompts for Section B
- read over the two texts you submitted for CBA 2
- make notes, if you wish

Step 2. Complete the Assessment Task booklet

During your next timetabled English class:

- your teacher will give you the booklet that you examined during the previous class
- you will complete the booklet on your own under exam conditions
- you will have your two written texts, which you can refer to as you answer the booklet

Section A of the booklet requires you to reflect on your texts. You will normally be asked to:

- write the title and genre of your written texts
- write a sample passage from one of your texts
- reflect on your use of features that are specific to the genre of your writing
- explain a change you made and how this change improved your written text

Section B of the booklet requires you to reflect on your writing experience. You will normally be asked to:

- choose two writing prompts from a list provided by your teacher, for example:
  - How the things I read helped me to be a better writer
  - How I worked with classmates as part of developing my writing skills
  - How a specific piece of feedback was useful to me
  - How I hope/would like to use my writing skills in the future
- respond to two of the prompts
- refer to the samples of your writing

MASTER THE LANGUAGE

Select one piece of writing that you have completed in this Learning Log.

(a) Write the title and genre of the written text that you have chosen.

Title: _____

Genre: _____

(b) Select an extract from the written text you have chosen and write it below. Ensure your chosen passage shows the quality of your writing.

_____
_____
_____
_____
_____
_____
_____
_____
_____

Louder than Words >> Learning Log

(c) Identify two features of the genre that you used in your writing.

| First feature: | |
| Second feature: | |

(d) Explain why these features are associated with the genre. Focus on the impact the features make on the writing overall and include examples from your writing.

(e) Identify a change you made to improve your writing and give one example from your writing.

The change I made was ...

Example:

(f) How did this change improve your writing?

_____
_____
_____
_____
_____
_____
_____
_____

Select two of the writing prompts below and write a response in the space provided.
- **(a)** How my own research helped me to become a better writer.
- **(b)** How working with others helped to improve my writing skills.
- **(c)** How I used feedback to make my writing better.
- **(d)** How I will approach writing tasks in the future.

Prompt ( ) _____
Response

_____
_____
_____
_____
_____
_____
_____
_____

Prompt ( ) _____
Response

_____
_____
_____
_____
_____
_____
_____
_____

Louder than Words >> Learning Log

Final Assessment

At the end of Third Year you will sit a two-hour written examination, which will assess the skills you have developed throughout the Junior Cycle English course.

Reading skills	Show your ability to read and engage with different texts by answering questions about them and discussing your thoughts and feelings.
Writing skills	Show that you can write in lots of different formats such as emails, letters and speeches. Show that you can write about and explore texts that you have studied such as novels, plays, films or poems.
English language skills	Show that you can identify and understand English language, punctuation and grammar such as identifying nouns, inserting apostrophes, explaining word meanings or discussing the features of a text, e.g. informal, friendly language is a feature of a diary entry.

The written exam will also test your knowledge and appreciation of the texts that you have studied in Second and Third Year.

Step 1. Familarise yourself with exam papers

It is essential to read the inside cover of the exam paper carefully, which contains information about the theme that connects the texts and questions, important information about the number of questions, how many marks each one is worth and how long you should spend answering each section, as well as some practical instructions.

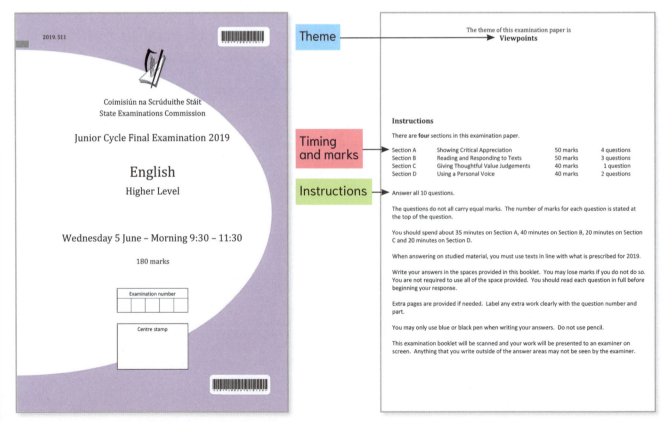

The **theme** of the exam is printed at the top of the inside cover of the exam paper. Although the themes are generally quite broad, all the texts, questions and tasks will relate to it in some way. For example, in 2019 the theme of the Higher Level paper was 'Viewpoints' and the theme of the Ordinary Level paper was 'Respect'. Get into the habit of finding the theme on the opening page of your exam, then spend a minute or two thinking about your understanding of the theme. Knowing the theme of the paper at the outset of the exam will provide you with a starting point for reading and understanding the material that follows.

 CHAT IT OUT

Can you think of any texts you have studied, literary and non-literary, that might fall under the theme of 'Viewpoints' or 'Respect'?

The layout of the exam is different each year. On the inside cover of the exam paper, you are told information about **timing and marks**:

- How many sections there are
- How many marks are allocated to each section
- How long you should spend on each section

This information is repeated at the start of each section in the paper.

You will also be told how many questions make up each section. Remember to check the clock when you begin each section.

Example

It is 10 a.m. You are starting Section B. The suggested time limit for Section B is 30 minutes. This means you must complete all questions in Section B by 10.30 a.m.

Each section has a heading, which tells you what you will be doing in that section. For example, in a 'Reading and Responding to Texts' section you will be reading texts and answering questions about them.

 MASTER THE LANGUAGE

There are no set headings for the sections in the exam, and they change from year to year. The following headings have appeared in previous years' exams. Match each heading to its meaning.

Responding to texts	Analysing the features of language, and thinking about the style of the text
Appreciating audience and register	Giving your own reaction to a text and creating something new and original
Responding to studied texts	Responding to functional tasks, writing something with a specific objective
Analysing visual imagery	Giving opinions on a text that you have never seen before
Responding imaginatively	Answering comprehension-style questions
Writing for a variety of purposes	Giving opinions, exploring characters and discussing texts you have looked at in class
Reading to understand	Exploring a visual text

Louder than Words >> Learning Log

Below the timing and marks there are **instructions**, which you must follow carefully in order to avoid losing marks. Directions may include:

- 'Write in the allocated space provided.'
- 'When answering on studied texts make sure to use the prescribed texts studied in class (from the prescribed list).'
- 'Write in blue or black pen only.'

When beginning a task in your exam, read the instruction carefully. Make sure you understand what the task demands of you. If a task requires you to answer a set of questions based on an extract or poem, it is helpful to skim through the questions before reading the extract. This will help you to pay attention to information that will be relevant to your answers.

Some tasks require prior thought and planning. You are provided with 'Optional Rough Work' space for some longer pieces of writing. This space can be used to write a short outline or plan for your work. All answers must be completed using the writing space provided within the examination paper.

Step 2. Understand what you are being asked

It is very important that you read each question carefully, answering exactly what you are asked. Remember that the examiner cannot give you marks if you go off-topic, so try to avoid summarising and stick to the question you see in front of you.

Though the English exam changes each year, questions are often asked in a similar way. Understanding the intentions of the following common words and phrases will help you figure out what you are expected to do.

Agree/Disagree	Give your opinion. It is very important that you support your point of view, backing it up with facts, reasons or quotes.
Analyse	Examine the details carefully in order to explain something.
Clarify	Make an idea or statement clear and easy to understand. It might help to rewrite the statement.
Comment	Discuss, explain or offer an opinion on something.
Compare	Look at two or more things in order to examine how they are similar or different.
Contrast	Look at two or more things in order to examine how they are different.
Define	Simply say exactly what something means.
Describe	Give clear details about what someone or something is like. Include sensory details such as the smell, sound, image, feeling and taste of something.
Discuss	Talk about something in detail. Take different ideas and opinions into account. Remember to back up your discussion points with facts, reasons and quotes.
Do you think / In your opinion	Share your view. You can say what you honestly think, providing reasons or quotes to back it up.
Evaluate	Assess the strengths and weaknesses of something. Talk about what you enjoyed about what you have read and what could be improved.
Explain	Make your answer clear by giving reasons for it and details about it.

Give an account	Write a detailed description of how or why something happened. Your own account of something should be written from your point of view.
Indicate	Show, make something clear or point something out.
Interpret	Find the meaning of something. Explain the meaning by sharing your personal outlook and giving examples.
Justify	Explain your opinion by providing reasons and evidence.
Outline	Give the main ideas or essential details without summarising or exploring something in great depth.
Prove	Provide evidence in order to prove that something is true.
State	Say something clearly.
With reference to	Mention details from the text and/or quote from it to support what you are saying.

You may be asked a question that includes a word you do not know straight away. You could also be asked to find the definition of a word from a list provided or to write the meaning in your own words. If you are asked the meaning of a word and feel unsure, don't panic – there are ways to figure it out.

- Usually, the words will be from an extract provided. Return to the extract and read the sentence that contains the word. Understanding the full sentence will help you to figure out the meaning of the word in question.
- Ask yourself if the word is a noun, verb, adjective or adverb:
  - If it is a noun, then it is a person, place, animal or thing. Reading the full sentence will help you narrow down which one.
  - If it is a verb, then you know it is an action – consider what is going on in the scene to figure out what the action might be.
  - If it is an adverb, look at the verb it is describing. Think about the character or setting/ atmosphere too. Does this tell you whether it is a positive or negative word?
  - If it is an adjective, look at the noun it is describing. Does this tell you if it is a positive or negative word? If it is describing a character, look for evidence of other character traits. For example, if the character is described as 'nasty, cruel and repugnant', the first two words 'nasty' and 'cruel' suggest that 'repugnant' is a word describing the character in a negative way.
- Try to break the word down. Understanding certain parts of the word may help you to piece it together.
  - For example, 'act' in words often means doing (e.g. action, react, interact), while 'pre' in words often means earlier or before (e.g. prepare, preamble).
  - Similarly, words with certain endings often have similar meanings. For example, words ending in 'ing' indicate action (e.g. dancing, singing, smiling), while words ending in 'holic' might show an obsession (e.g. workaholic, shopaholic).
- Examine the sound of the word, which might lead you towards the meaning.
- Do you know a similar word that might help you work it out?

Louder than Words >> Learning Log

Follow these steps to identify the purpose of each question:

1. Read the question three times and ask yourself 'What am I being asked to do?'
2. Underline the most important words in the question
3. Try to work out the meaning of any words you do not know.

Example

Do you think that the writer of this article uses language effectively to convey her views to the reader? Explain your answer with reference to the article.

1. Having read this question three times, I understand that it is asking me to comment on how and how well the writer of the article uses language to put across her opinion to the audience. I must refer to the article in my answer.

2. Do you <u>think</u> that the writer of this article uses <u>language effectively</u> to <u>convey her views</u> to the reader? <u>Explain</u> your answer with <u>reference</u> to the article.

   Underlining these important words makes it clear what the examiner is looking for in my answer: I must explain my opinion of how the writer uses effective language to make her ideas clear.

3. In this question, the most challenging words for me are:
   - Effectively: to do something well or successfully
     – Does the writer use language in a successful way?
     – Is her message clear?
   - Convey: to show or communicate something
     – What are the writer's views?
     – Is the writer's message easy to understand?
   - Reference: to refer to something or discuss it
     – What examples could you give from the extract?
     – Could you include quotes to show examples of the writer's effective language?

MASTER THE LANGUAGE

Follow the steps outlined above to work out the purpose of questions 1 and 2 below.
1. Write a descriptive passage set in an interesting place.
2. What aspects of the poem would make it suitable for dramatisation? Explain your answer with reference to the poem.

👥 Compare your understanding of both questions with a partner.

When you come to write your answer, remember to take the following steps:

1. Refer to the question and answer it in your own words. Link back to the question asked by using words from it. Begin the answer to the question with a statement.
2. Use evidence from the text to support your answer. Remember to use quotation marks when quoting directly from the text.
3. Explain how your evidence answers the question.

Step 3. Keep in mind what the examiner is looking for

The examiner will use Indicators of Quality in order to see if you have done everything that was asked. They will be looking out for the following when assessing the quality of your answers.

Focus	Answer the question that you are asked, remain focused.
Ideas	Explore ideas and interpretations in an original way. Express your ideas to the best of your ability.
Development	Develop your answers in depth and support your point of view with evidence such as quotation.
Coherence	Stay on-task, structure your answers using paragraphs and organise your writing in a clear and meaningful way.
Expression	Write to the best of your ability, using clear language. Avoid writing very long sentences.
Register	Your language should match the task. Formal language may be used in an email or letter of complaint while informal language may be used in a blog.
Creativity	Show an ability to think and write creatively where possible.
Spelling and punctuation	Work hard to spell each word correctly. Make accurate use of punctuation, especially apostrophes.

Step 4. Practise, practise, practise!

The best way to prepare for your written paper is to practise answering exam questions. You have been answering exam-style and past paper questions in the course of using *Louder than Words*. Review your answers to the questions and compare your answers to any sample answers provided.

It is also useful to look at sample papers and past exam papers. The following tables point you towards the papers and questions to look at to practise answering on different genres.

Ordinary Level
Questions on studied novels

SEC Examination Paper 2018 Freedom	Section B Q.8
SEC Examination Paper 2019 Respect	Section B Q.10

Questions on studied drama or film

SEC Examination Paper 2017 Following Your Passions	Section A Q.3
SEC Examination Paper 2018 Freedom	Section D Q.13
SEC Examination Paper 2019 Respect	Section B Q.10

Questions on studied poetry

SEC Sample Paper 1 Young People and the World	Section C Q.14
SEC Examination Paper 2017 Following Your Passions	Section D Q.15
SEC Examination Paper 2018 Freedom	Section A Q.4

Louder than Words » Learning Log

Responding to unseen poetry

SEC Sample Paper 1 Young People and the World	Section C Q.9, Q.11, Q.12
SEC Examination Paper 2017 Following Your Passions	Section D Q.13, Q.14
SEC Examination Paper 2018 Freedom	Section A Q.1, Q.2

Responding to unseen texts, fiction and non-fiction

SEC Sample Paper 1 Young People and the World	Section A Q.1, Q.2, Q.3, Q.4, Q.5, Q.6
SEC Examination Paper 2017 Following Your Passions	Section A Q.1, Q.2 Section B Q.4, Q.5, Q.6, Q.7, Q.8 Section C Q.9, Q.10
SEC Examination Paper 2018 Freedom	Section B Q.5, Q.6, Q.8
SEC Examination Paper 2019 Respect	Section A Q.1, Q.2, Q.3, Q.4 Section B Q.6, Q.7, Q.8, Q.10 Section C Q.11, Q.12

Writing and composing questions

SEC Sample Paper 1 Young People and the World	Section B Q.7 Section C Q.13
SEC Examination Paper 2017 Following Your Passions	Section B Q.7 Section C Q.11, Q.12 Section D Q.16 (c)
SEC Examination Paper 2018 Freedom	Section A Q.3 Section B Q.7, Q.9, Q.10, Q.11 Section D Q.14
SEC Examination Paper 2019 Respect	Section A Q.5 Section B Q.9 Section C Q.15

Language questions

SEC Sample Paper 1 Young People and the World	Section C Q.10
SEC Examination Paper 2018 Freedom	Section C Q.12
SEC Examination Paper 2019 Respect	Section C Q.14

Higher Level
Questions on studied novels

SEC Sample Paper 2 Making Connections	Section B Q.10
SEC Sample Paper 3 A Sense of Place	Section B Q.3, Q.4
SEC Examination Paper 2019 Viewpoints	Section B Q.7
SEC Examination Paper 2018 Appearance and Reality	Section B Q.5

Questions on studied drama or film

SEC Sample Paper 2 Making Connections	Section A Q.5
SEC Examination Paper 2019 Viewpoints	Section C Q.8
SEC Examination Paper 2018 Appearance and Reality	Section C Q.8
SEC Examination Paper 2017 Mysteries	Section C Q.7, Q.8, Q.9

Questions on studied poetry

SEC Sample Paper 3 A Sense of Place	Section D Q.11
SEC Examination Paper 2019 Viewpoints	Section A Q.4
SEC Examination Paper 2017 Mysteries	Section B Q.3

Responding to unseen poetry

SEC Sample Paper 3 A Sense of Place	Section D Q.8, Q.9, Q.10
SEC Examination Paper 2019 Viewpoints	Section A Q.1, Q.2, Q.3
SEC Examination Paper 2018 Appearance and Reality	Section C Q.9

Responding to unseen drama

| SEC Examination Paper 2017 Mysteries | Section C Q.5, Q.6 |

Responding to unseen texts, fiction and non-fiction

SEC Sample Paper 2 Making Connections	Section A Q.1, Q.2, Q.3, Q.4 Section B Q.6, Q.7, Q.9
SEC Sample Paper 3 A Sense of Place	Section A Q.1 Section C Q.5, Q.6
SEC Examination Paper 2019 Viewpoints	Section B Q.5, Q.6 Section D Q.9
SEC Examination Paper 2018 Appearance and Reality	Section A Q.1, Q.3,
SEC Examination Paper 2017 Mysteries	Section A Q.1, Q.2

Writing and composing questions

SEC Sample Paper 2 Making Connections	Section B Q.11
SEC Sample Paper 3 A Sense of Place	Section A Q.2 Section C Q.7 Section D Q.12
SEC Examination Paper 2019 Viewpoints	Section D Q.10
SEC Examination Paper 2018 Appearance and Reality	Section A Q.4 Section B Q.6
SEC Examination Paper 2017 Mysteries	Section D Q.10

Louder than Words >> Learning Log

Language questions

SEC Sample Paper 2 Making Connections	Section B Q.8
SEC Examination Paper 2018 Appearance and Reality	Section A Q.2 Section B Q.7
SEC Examination Paper 2017 Mysteries	Section B Q.4

Exam advice

- **Know your studied texts:** Be able to quote from them, talk about characters, refer to techniques and discuss key moments. Form your own opinion of each text and poem before the exam, that way you can easily discuss your favourite moment or character.
- **Stay calm:** On the day of your exam, try to be confident. Remember that it is an opportunity to show off the skills you have been building. Work calmly and carefully, aiming to complete your exam in full. Answer all questions in order to achieve the best mark possible.
- **Watch the clock:** Pay attention to time and if you run out of time in a particular section, finish your sentence and move on. You might have time at the end to go back and finish it. Be strict with yourself, stick to the time given for each section of your exam.
- **Pay attention to marks:** Keep an eye on the marks for each question. Avoid writing short answers for long questions or long answers for short questions. Use the answer space provided, get to the point, develop it fully and move on.
- **Use a blue or black pen:** Remember that your exam will be scanned and marked by an examiner who will read your answers online. Only blue and black ink will be clearly visible on-screen.
- **Attempt everything:** Answer all questions. Remember, there are no marks for blank spaces!

Question 4, 2018 Ordinary Level (20 marks)

Choose a poem you have studied (from Studied Poet 1: Maya Angelou on pages 150–160 of your textbook) where the poet expresses a strong feeling about something he or she has experienced.

Optional rough work

(a) Title of poem:

(b) Name of poet:

(c) What was the poet feeling?

(d) Why do you think the poet was feeling that way?

Louder than Words >> Learning Log

(e) Did you think the poet had chosen a good title for his or her poem? Give a reason for your answer.

(f) Did you like or dislike the poem you have chosen? Explain your answer.

Questions 4–7, 2017 Ordinary Level (30 marks)

Read the following extract from the graphic novel *American Born Chinese* by Gene Luen Yang.

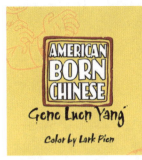

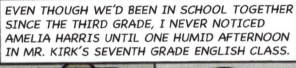

Louder than Words >> Learning Log

Question 4 (10 marks)

Describe what happens in the first four frames of this story.

Optional rough work

Question 5 (5 marks)

Look at frames 8 and 9. Which one of the following two words do you think best describes Wei-Chen's reaction when Jin tells him about Amelia?

- Mean

    or

- Funny

Give a reason for your answer.

Question 6 (10 marks)

Look at the next frame in the story which shows Jin lying in bed the night he has discovered that his friend Wei-Chen now has a girlfriend. Fill in the thought box with what you think Jin may have been thinking.

Optional rough work

Louder than Words >> Learning Log

Question 7 (5 marks)

This is an extract from a graphic novel. Graphic novels use a mixture of pictures and text to tell a story. Do you like this way of telling a story? Give a reason for your answer.

Louder than Words >> Learning Log

Question 3, 2017 Higher Level (40 marks)

(a) *'The more familiar you become with a poem, the deeper your understanding of that poem becomes.'*

Select a poem you have studied (from Studied Poet 2: Seamus Heaney on pages 318–329 of your textbook) and explain how this statement applies to your understanding of this poem. Use the poem to support your ideas.

Optional rough work

Title of poem:

Name of poet:

Louder than Words » Learning Log

(b) Identify at least two poetic techniques used in your chosen poem and explain how the poet makes effective use of these techniques in this poem. Support your ideas with reference to the poem.

Optional rough work

Louder than Words >> Learning Log

(20 marks)

The song 'Anseo' by Denise Chaila on page 343 of your textbook includes a speaker with a strong voice and sense of self. Choose a poem you have studied that features a strong voice.

Optional rough work

Title of poem:

Name of poet:

(a) Describe the person or character behind the voice in the poem. (5 marks)

(b) What kind of tone is behind the voice in this poem? Give an example from the poem to illustrate your answer. (5 marks)

(c) Choose one poetic device from this poem and explain how it helps you to understand the voice in the poem and what they are saying. (10 marks)

Device:

Explanation:

Louder than Words >> Learning Log

(20 marks)

From a play you have studied, choose a moment where a character's true identity is revealed. Describe the revelation of the character's true identity and explain how it affects the outcome of the play.

                  Optional rough work

I studied the play _____ by _____
_____ and the scene I have chosen where a character's identity is revealed is

----
| |
| |

Describe the revelation.

| |
| |
| |
| |
| |
| |
| |
| |
| |
| |
| |
| |

How does it affect the outcome of the play?

Louder than Words >> Learning Log

(20 marks)

Choose a relationship from a play or film you have studied and explain why you think it is a strong relationship.

Optional rough work

(10 marks)

Choose two poetic devices from the poem 'How to Come Out as Gay' by Dean Atta on page 361 of your textbook and explain how effective they are in conveying the intended message.

Device 1:

Explanation:

Device 2:

Explanation:

Louder than Words >> Learning Log

1. Who do the following pronouns refer to? Match the pairs. (3 marks)

He
She
They

Non-binary person (singular)
Woman
Man

2. Fill in the gaps in the following sentences using gender-neutral pronouns. (10 marks)

Example

*Helen couldn't believe **their** eyes when **they** saw what lay ahead of **them**.*

   (a) Robyn felt uncertain and didn't know if _____ were making the right decision.

   (b) Jack couldn't eat _____ breakfast because _____ were anxious about _____ exams.

   (c) Alex started cycling to school when _____ got a new bike for _____ birthday.

   (d) Sam hoped _____ mum would understand why _____ arrived home late despite the warning she had given _____.

   (e) Tash loved going for walks alone and spending time by _____.

(a) Suggest an alternative title for the short story 'Trial by Combat' by Shirley Jackson on page 379 of your textbook. Give reasons for your answer. (5 marks)

(b) Would you like to live in this rooming house? Explain your answer. (10 marks)

Louder than Words >> Learning Log

(c) Choose one of the following words to describe Mrs Allen's character. Explain your choice with reference to the story (10 marks)

Stubborn   Lonely   Dishonest   Cruel

Chosen word

Reason 1:

Reason 2:

3 » Fire Ahead with Assessment

(20 marks)

Choose a novel or short story you have studied where a character has power over another character or characters.

Optional rough work

Title of novel/short story:

Name of character:

(a) Describe the scene where this power is evident.

(b) How does the character gain power over the other character(s)?

Louder than Words >> Learning Log

The poem 'Invictus' by William Ernest Henley on page 394 of your textbook has a powerful message.

Optional rough work

(a) What do you think is the message of the poem? (5 marks)

(b) How does the poet use language to effectively convey this message? (10 marks)

Poetic device:

Explanation:

1. In your opinion, which of the following images do you think best represents the central message of the poem 'Standing' by Carol Kinane on page 397 of your textbook? (5 marks)

Image 1

Image 2

Chosen image:

Give two reasons for your answer using support from the poem.

Reason 1:

Reason 2:

2. In the space below, outline the plot of a short story that captures the theme of 'powerlessness'. (10 marks)

Louder than Words >> Learning Log

Answer the following questions about the extract from *When Hitler Stole Pink Rabbit* by Judith Kerr on page 400 of your textbook. (9 marks)

1. What is the name of the building where the German Parliament met? Place the correct letter in the box provided.

    (a) The Brandenburg Gate

    (b) The Reichstag

    (c) The Rotes Rathaus

2. What is the name of Anna's teacher? Place the correct letter in the box provided.

    (a) Fräulein Schulz

    (b) Fräulein Schneider

    (c) Fräulein Schmidt

3. At the end of the extract Anna says 'the taxi went round the corner and it all disappeared'. What does she mean? Place the correct letter in the box provided.

    (a) Anna means that her home disappeared from view

    (b) Anna means that Germany disappeared from view

    (c) Anna means that her toys disappeared from view

4. Suggest words to describe how Anna and Max may be feeling as they leave their home behind. Write your words in the spaces provided.

Louder than Words » Learning Log

1. Imagine you are reviewing the extract from *The Boxer* by Nikesh Shukla on page 407 of your textbook.

   (a) Choose one of the following words which best characterises the extract in your view and explain your choice. (10 marks)

   Tense   Exciting   Dramatic

Chosen word:

Example 1:

Example 2:

   (b) Imagine you are a director bringing this extract to life on screen. Explain two directions that you would give to the actor playing Sunny. (10 marks)

Direction 1:

Direction 2:

3 ›› Fire Ahead with Assessment

2. From a novel you have studied, choose a character who is unfairly treated by another character or characters.

Optional rough work

Name the character who is unfairly treated:

Describe a key moment in the story where this unfair treatment is evident. (10 marks)

Louder than Words >> Learning Log

The scene from *The Alternative* by Michael Patrick and Oisín Kearney on page 435 of your textbook is an example of people having opposing viewpoints.

Choose a text that you have studied where people have opposing viewpoints.

Optional rough work

Name of text:

Name of author:

(a) What are the opposing viewpoints? (5 marks)

(b) Describe a scene from the text where these opposing viewpoints are most evident. (10 marks)

(20 marks)

Choose a character from a novel you have studied that you admire.

Imagine you have the opportunity to invite this character into your school to speak to your classmates. Write the text of the speech you would make to your classmates to introduce this character, explaining why you admire them.

Optional rough work

Name of character:

Name of novel:

Louder than Words >> Learning Log

Answer the following questions about the poem 'crying' by Hollie McNish on page 464 of your textbook.

(a) What evidence is there to suggest that the poet thinks it is okay to cry? (5 marks)

(b) Do you think young people today feel they can express their feelings freely? Explain your point of view. (5 marks)

(c) The poet sets the scene at the end of the poem by providing a shoulder to cry on. Write the dialogue that you imagine takes place between the speaker and the person crying. (10 marks)

Optional rough work

Louder than Words » Learning Log

Answer the following questions about the poem 'be the best' by Hollie McNish on page 468 of your textbook.

(a) You have been asked to select a poem that would appeal to young people like you. Explain why 'be the best' would be a good choice. (10 marks)

(b) Do you think young people are under pressure to be the best? Tick the box to show your opinion.

Yes ☐   No ☐   Sometimes ☐

Explain your answer. (10 marks)

(c) What advice does the poet give her readers? Explain why this advice is or is not helpful. (10 marks)

Louder than Words >> Learning Log

Answer the following questions about the poem 'fill your basket' by Hollie McNish on page 472 of your textbook. (20 marks)

(a) The poem 'fill your basket' has an important message. What important message is expressed in the poem?

(b) How does the poet use language to express the message you have identified? You should refer to poetic devices such as imagery, alliteration and metaphor.

3 >> Fire Ahead with Assessment

Answer the following questions about the poetry of Hollie McNish on pages 463–478 of your textbook.

1. Select two poems that you have studied by the same poet and compare the poems under the headings provided. (20 marks)

Name of first poem:

Name of second poem:

(a) Themes

(b) Imagery

(c) Your favourite aspect of both poems

(d) The poem you enjoyed most

(40 marks)

2. *Poems can teach us important lessons.*

Write about a poem that you have studied which taught you an important lesson.

Name of poem:

Name of poet:

(a) What important lesson did you learn?

(b) How does the poet use language to get their message or lesson across?

(c) Write a blog post about the poem that you have studied.

Additional Writing Space